Candlemaking
the Natural Way

Candlemaking the Natural Way

31 Projects Made with Soy, Palm & Beeswax

REBECCA ITTNER

LARK
CRAFTS

A Division of Sterling Publishing Co., Inc.
New York / London

A Red Lips 4 Courage
Communications, Inc. book

www.redlips4courage.com

Eileen Cannon Paulin
President

Catherine Risling
Director of Editorial

Erika Kotite
Development Director

Art Director: Susan H. Hartman

Copy Editors: Erika Kotite,
Catherine Risling

Photographer: Mark Tanner

Photo Stylist: Rebecca Ittner

Library of Congress Cataloging-in-Publication Data

Ittner, Rebecca.
  Candlemaking the natural way : 31 projects made with soy, palm & beeswax
/ Rebecca Ittner. -- 1st ed.
      p. cm.
  Includes index.
  ISBN 978-1-60059-600-1 (hc-plc with jacket : alk. paper)
  1. Candlemaking. I. Title.
  TT896.5.I88 2010
  745.593'32--dc22

                                        2009049876

10 9 8 7 6 5 4 3 2 1

First Edition

Published by Lark Crafts, A Division of Sterling Publishing Co., Inc.
387 Park Avenue South, New York, NY 10016
New York / London

Text © 2010, Rebecca Ittner
Photography © 2010, Red Lips 4 Courage Communications, Inc.
Illustrations © 2010, Red Lips 4 Courage Communications, Inc.

Distributed in Canada by Sterling Publishing,
c/o Canadian Manda Group, 165 Dufferin Street
Toronto, Ontario, Canada M6K 3H6

Distributed in the United Kingdom by GMC Distribution Services,
Castle Place, 166 High Street, Lewes, East Sussex, England BN7 1XU

Distributed in Australia by Capricorn Link (Australia) Pty Ltd.,
P.O. Box 704, Windsor, NSW 2756 Australia

If you have questions or comments about this book, please contact:

Lark Crafts
67 Broadway
Asheville, NC 28801
(828) 253-0467

Manufactured in China

ISBN 13: 978-1-60059-600-1

For information about custom editions, special sales, premium and
corporate purchases, please contact Sterling Special Sales Department
at (800) 805-5489 or specialsales@sterlingpub.com.

For information about desk and examination copies available to college and
university professors, requests must be submitted to academic@larkbooks.com.
Our complete policy can be found at www.larkbooks.com.

CONTENTS

INTRODUCTION

Candles were born out of necessity, centuries before electricity. We may no longer need them as our main source of light, but candles continue to hold a special place in our lives. We use them to mark celebrations, decorate our homes, set a romantic mood, and influence emotions.

Candlemaking is still a popular craft and one that changes with the times. As the demand for natural products continues to grow, crafters are looking for earth-friendly options to use in their candle projects. Happily, there are wonderful natural waxes available that can be used to create all types of candles, from votives and pillars to molded and container candles. In this book, I focus on the three most common natural waxes: beeswax, soy wax, and palm wax.

Beeswax is the original "green" candle wax and has been used to make candles for centuries. A natural byproduct of honey production, honeybees produce beeswax to build honeycomb. Its golden color and wonderful scent comes from the honey, pollen, and propolis (a waxy substance that comes from buds) that mix in the hive.

Soy wax was the invention of Michael Richards, who saw a demand for a natural wax in addition to beeswax and one that would be cost-competitive with paraffin. Beginning in the early 1990s, Richards spent years experimenting with natural waxes and oils before he perfected his soy wax formula around 1999. In its natural state, soy wax is white and soft and perfect for container candles. With natural additives, the wax can be used for pillars, tapers, and molded candles.

Around the time Richards was experimenting with soy wax in the United States, palm wax was being developed on the other side of the globe. Within a decade, eco-conscious crafters had two new, and very different, waxes to work with. Palm wax has a big personality. Where beeswax and soy wax candles are naturally smooth, a palm wax candle has beautiful crystallized patterns on its surface. Unlike soy wax, palm wax needs no additives for use in pillar and molded candles.

Though there is a variety of natural waxes, there are no truly natural candle dyes. Essential oils are a natural way to scent candles, but the range of scents is limited. Because of these limitations, the candles in this book were made using natural waxes and a variety of dyes and scents. If the candles were purely natural, they would all be cream or white and smell like flowers or botanicals! Instead, you'll find candles of differing shapes and sizes, made using a wide variety of colors, scents, and techniques.

You will learn the basics of candlemaking, such as simple molded and rolled pillars and container candles, as well as a few more advanced projects like hand-molded beeswax shapes and embedded candles. With time and patience, even the beginning candle crafter can successfully make all of them, benefitting from the amazing talent of candle artists who contributed the many projects in this book.

Rebekah Ashley used her artistic gifts to create unique painted palm wax candles. While most candle crafters add dye to melted wax, Rebekah painted liquid wax inside her molds to achieve amazing results. In another project, her layered candles were painted with colored stearin and smell divine.

Paoling Che made beeswax candles in a variety of shapes and sizes, from incredible hand-shaped roses to potted beeswax grass and simple molded hearts and flowers. Cathie Filian took rolled beeswax candles to the next level. Her cookie cutter pillars are stunning, yet surprisingly easy to create. Melissa Kotz made an amazing layered palm wax candle that was inspired by the colors of a piece of pottery.

Angie Rodriguez contributed both soy wax and palm wax projects. Her techniques to create chunky candles work well with both types of wax. Angie's Exotic Peach soy wax candles and Celestial palm wax candles are colorful and exciting.

Cheryl Murakami has a way with beeswax sheets; her rolled hearts are perfect for wedding favors. Patrick Troxell's layered pillars brighten any table. Sara Werzel's simple molded pillars are perfect for the beginning candlemaker.

As you gather tools and supplies to make your own candles, think outside of the box. In keeping with the eco-friendly theme, remember to reuse and recycle. When possible, use what you have. Cover work surfaces, including the floor, with newspaper. Set candles to cool on old baking sheets that are too damaged for food use. Create shaped candles with discarded cookie cutters or silicone baking cups. Pour leftover wax into clean glass food jars. Use orphaned teacups, bowls, and vintage glass candy jars for container candles. Set a picnic table with shell candles to celebrate summer. Decorate a mantel with a trio of painted candles. Melt old candles and layer the colors to create personalized gifts or pour the wax into small tins to create travel candles.

After completing the projects on the following pages, I hope you are inspired to continue your candlemaking journey. With time and imagination, the possibilities are endless.

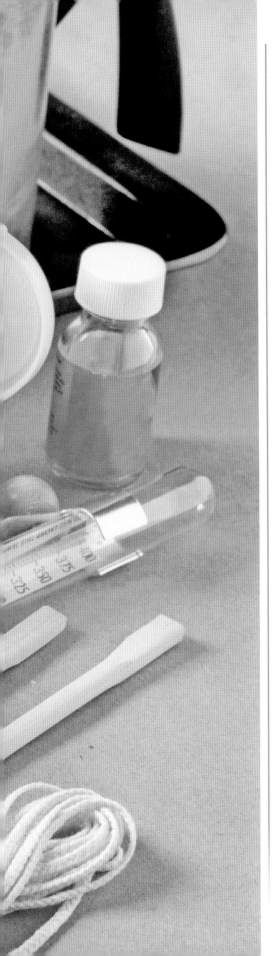

CHAPTER 1

Getting Started

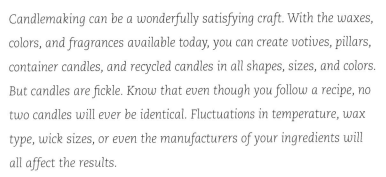

Candlemaking can be a wonderfully satisfying craft. With the waxes, colors, and fragrances available today, you can create votives, pillars, container candles, and recycled candles in all shapes, sizes, and colors. But candles are fickle. Know that even though you follow a recipe, no two candles will ever be identical. Fluctuations in temperature, wax type, wick sizes, or even the manufacturers of your ingredients will all affect the results.

Many times these differences are happy accidents; other times they are frustrating. One of the most important things you can do is keep a detailed diary of your candlemaking journey. Use it to record things like the type, manufacturer, and amount of wax, wicks, fragrance, and colorants used; melting and pouring temperatures; and cooling times.

In this chapter you will learn the basic differences between paraffin and natural waxes, the tools and materials needed to make the candles in this book, and basic safety tips. Once you familiarize yourself with these and learn the simple techniques in the following chapter, you will be ready to start candle crafting.

11

NATURAL VS. SYNTHETIC

For many years, paraffin has been the wax of choice for both commercial and home-based candle crafters. For those who wanted to make natural candles, beeswax was the only answer. In recent years, however, soy wax and palm wax have come to market, and with them a whole new realm of candlemaking possibilities.

But why choose natural? Natural waxes are biodegradable and come from renewable resources. There are additional benefits to using natural waxes and these are discussed in the following chapter openers in this book. Paraffin, on the other hand, is a petroleum byproduct.

Choosing natural waxes is a personal decision, one most often driven by a desire to avoid synthetic, petroleum-based products and to use waxes that are eco-friendly.

MATERIALS AND TOOLS

Much of what is needed to make candles can be found in your kitchen. Everything else is readily available at craft and cookware stores. Once you use an item for candlemaking, it should not be used for cooking; wax, fragrance, and colorants can be transferred back into food. Consider storing your candlemaking supplies in marked boxes to prevent any cross-contamination.

THE BASICS

- **Candle or candy thermometer:** Used to measure wax temperature.
- **Chisel or flathead screwdriver:** Used to break up blocks of wax.
- **Craft knife:** Used to cut beeswax sheets.
- **Cutting board:** Plastic or wood; used to chop or break up blocks of wax.
- **Double boiler or melting pot:** Used to melt wax.
- **Glass measuring cup:** Used to measure and pour wax.
- **Kitchen scale:** Used to weigh wax.
- **Kitchen towels:** Used to wipe condensation off the bottom of the double boiler or melting pot.
- **Knives:** Large and paring; used to cut wax into chunks and trim excess wax from molded candles.
- **Measuring spoons:** Used to measure additives.
- **Metal spoon:** Used for stirring additives into wax.

PLAYING IT SAFE

There are a few simple rules to ensure that candle crafting is a safe activity. Some basics include:

Never melt wax over direct heat. Wax is flammable and will catch fire. Never try to extinguish a wax fire with water; it will fuel the flame. Use baking soda, a saucepan lid, or fire blanket to contain a wax fire. Consider having a fire extinguisher on hand.

Never leave melting wax unattended. Also, to avoid a fire hazard make sure there is water in the bottom pan of your double boiler at all times.

Use pot holders or wear oven mitts or silicone gloves when pouring wax to prevent burns.

Never leave burning candles unattended or burn candles near things that are flammable, such as curtains, plants, or paper décor.

- **Mold sealer:** Used to seal the wick hole in a mold and prevent wax from leaking.

- **Molds:** Used to create shaped candles.

- **Newspaper:** Used to cover the work surface and protect it from wax.

- **Oven gloves:** Used to prevent burns from hot wax.

- **Paper towels:** Used to clean up spills and other messes.

- **Parchment paper or wax paper:** Used to collect wax so it can be reused.

- **Pouring container:** Used for pouring wax.

- **Rubber mallet:** Used with chisel or flathead screwdriver to break up blocks of wax.

- **Scissors or nail clippers:** Used to trim wicks.

- **Self-healing cutting mat:** Used with craft knife to cut beeswax sheets.

Containers and Molds

The vessel you choose for a container candle should be based on the type of candle. If you are making a layered candle, you will need a clear container. If you are reusing old wax, then a pretty china container would work well. Make sure your containers are heatproof so they do not crack or break when the wax is poured.

Candles can be made from a variety of molds, from pre-made metal molds to silicone baking pans. Here are some common types of molds:

Baking molds: Metal cake molds, cookie cutters, and silicone baking items such as cupcake and muffin molds.

Metal candle molds: Available in a wide range of sizes and shapes. Long-wearing.

Plastic candle molds: Typically two-piece molds. Some require use of mold clamps and mold stands.

Soft candle molds: Made from latex or silicone, candles are easily removed from these flexible molds.

Natural Wax

Currently, three types of natural wax are widely available: beeswax, soy wax, and palm wax. Each type has distinct properties, so making candles is slightly different with each one.

BEESWAX

Beeswax is a natural byproduct of honey production. It is filtered and purified before being packaged for use in candlemaking. Beeswax is heavy and sticky, so it can be hard to remove from some intricate molds. Molds that work well with beeswax include flexible silicone molds, two-piece molds that are easy to separate, and small metal molds.

Beeswax is readily available in three forms: pellets (also called pastilles), pre-made sheets, and 1- and 2-lb. (454 and 908 g) blocks; larger quantities can be found online. Pellets are used to make tapers, votives, pillars, and molded candles, and are easy to weigh and work with in comparison to the blocks. Beeswax sheets are commonly sold in 8 × 16-inch (20.3 × 40.6 cm) sheets and are used to make rolled and stacked candles. Beeswax blocks are the easiest to find, but must be broken up prior to use. I have the best luck using a rubber mallet and chisel or straight-edged screwdriver to break up blocks of beeswax.

PALM WAX

Palm wax is sold in flake form. Though not widely available in craft stores, many online sellers offer palm wax. There are different formulations of palm wax depending on the type of candle you want to make. The most common formulations are: crystallizing container wax, crystallizing votive/pillar wax, feathering pillar wax, and palm stearin. Palm stearin is a wax additive that increases burn time and firmness, and aids in mold release.

SOY WAX

Soy wax is also sold in flake form. For the casual crafter, 1- and 4-lb. (454 and 1816 g) packages are sold in craft stores. Larger quantities can be purchased from online sellers. In its most natural state, soy wax is a very soft wax that's best used only for container candles. Other formulations contain additives, such as palm stearin, that harden the wax and make it suitable for use in making votives, tapers, pillars, and molded candles. These formulations are referred to as either container formula or votive/pillar formula.

Wax Fragrances

Scent has the ability to influence a person's mood, a room's ambiance, and even the taste of food. For instance, lavender and vanilla are calming, jasmine and clary sage are uplifting, and mandarin orange is invigorating. If you plan to use a candle as a centerpiece for a dinner table, consider leaving it unscented so it won't compete with the aromas of the food being served. Unscented candles are also a great option for people with allergies to fragrance.

There are a couple of choices when it comes to scenting your candles: essential oils and fragrance oils. Essential oils are extracted from plants, shrubs, roots, bark, flowers, peelings, and resins, and are the only truly natural way to scent candles. You can use one oil or create a blend of oils to scent your candle; there are no rules.

Creating essential oil blends is a personal journey. Essential oils can be broken down two ways: by scent family and by notes. Understanding what scent family a particular essential oil belongs to will help you build a fragrance recipe. For instance, if you want to add a woodsy note to an herbal blend, refer to the list of scent families (at left). Understanding what note category an essential oil belongs to will help you create balanced essential oil blends (see Fragrance Notes, opposite page). Top notes are the main scent of the blend, middle notes enhance top notes, and base notes give depth to the blend. Information about essential oil blending abounds in books and on the Internet. The only way to know how a blend will make a candle smell is by experimenting. Taking notes as

SCENT FAMILIES

Floral	Herbal
jasmine	chamomile
lavender	clary sage
neroli	eucalyptus
rose	peppermint
ylang-ylang	rosemary

Spice	Citrus
black pepper	bergamot
cinnamon	grapefruit
coriander	lemon
ginger	lime
nutmeg	orange (sweet)
vanilla	tangerine

Earthy	Woodsy
frankincense	cedarwood
myrrh	sandalwood
patchouli	
vetiver	

you blend and again when you burn the candle will allow you to recreate the fragrance or let you know what doesn't work.

Fragrance oils can be a blend of essential and synthetic oils or purely synthetic. The advantage of fragrance oils is the wide range of scents available including things like pumpkin pie and chocolate. It is important to use only fragrance oils made specifically for scenting candles. These fragrance oils are designed to be fully absorbed by the wax and won't adversely affect how the candle burns. The projects in this book were scented using both natural essential oils and synthetic fragrance oils.

Wax Dyes

Though natural waxes are widely available, there are no truly natural dyes. Recently, a few eco-friendly liquid dyes have become available on the market. Because of the limited availability of these dyes, the projects in this book are made using a variety of dyes, both traditional and eco-friendly.

To ensure that your candles burn safely and well, use only dyes designated for candlemaking. Food coloring should not be used; they are water-based colors and will not mix with the wax. Crayons also should

FRAGRANCE NOTES

Top notes

bergamot	neroli
clary sage	orange
coriander	peppermint
eucalyptus	sage
grapefruit	spearmint
lemon	tea tree
lemongrass	thyme
lime	verbena
mandarin/ tangerine	

Middle notes

bergamot	lavender
black pepper	lemongrass
chamomile	neroli
coriander	nutmeg
cypress	pine
geranium	rosemary

Base notes

cedarwood	neroli
cinnamon	patchouli
clove	rose
frankincense	sandalwood
ginger	vetiver
jasmine	ylang-ylang
myrrh	

not be used. Though they are made using paraffin wax, other elements of the crayon can clog a wick and cause the candle to burn incorrectly. Types of candle dyes available:

Dye blocks and chips: Made of heavily dyed wax.

Liquid dye: More concentrated than dye blocks or chips.

Powder dye: The most concentrated of candle dyes. (The amount of powder that would fit on the tip of a toothpick would color a large candle.)

Wicks, Wick Accessories, and Wick Tools

Choosing the correct wick size and type is key to creating successful candles. It can be a time-consuming process, but your effort will be rewarded each time you light a candle that burns correctly. There is no sure-fire method to choosing wicks; there is a lot of trial and error and testing, testing, testing. Keeping a detailed journal about your wicking experimentation will help you determine what works and what does not.

The most common types of wicks include:

Cored wicks: Braided or knitted wicks with a core that helps keep the wick upright while burning. Common core ingredients are cotton, paper, tin, or zinc. Used in floating candles, jar candles, pillars, and votives.

Flat wicks: Braided, plaited, or knitted wicks that curl in the candle flame for a self-trimming benefit. Flat, braided wicks are the most common type of wick for taper and pillar candles.

Square wicks: Braided or knitted wicks that are also self-trimming, square wicks are more rounded and a bit thicker than flat wicks. Great for all types of candles as they can help prevent clogging of the wick.

There are also specialty wicks for use with certain types of wax, including palm and soy wax. Though not widely available, you may wish to try these in your candles. An Internet search for "soy candle wicks" or "palm candle wicks" will yield information on companies that provide them.

In addition to choosing the correct type of wick, it is important to select the proper size wick for your candle. Choose the wrong size and the wick may be snuffed out by a pool of wax (caused by using too small of a wick), or the candle will smoke and wax may run down the sides (caused by using too large of a wick). Wick is sized by its ply, or number of threads that are braided or spun together. The size or ply you choose is determined by the size of the candle you will be pouring; the larger the diameter of the candle, the larger ply of wick you will need.

Wick ply is different for each type of wick and may vary by manufacturer. Follow manufacturer recommendations to start, then adjust the size and type as needed according to your candle-testing results.

Additional Tools

In addition to the wick, you will need the following:

- **Adhesive wax:** Used to hold wick tabs in place.

- **Mold sealer:** Used to seal the wick hole and hold wicks in place.

- **Pliers:** Used to clamp wick tabs closed.

- **Votive wick pin:** Used to create a wick hole in votive candles and to pierce holes in beeswax shapes.

- **Wick holders:** Include wick sticks, wooden chopsticks or skewers, toothpicks, and cocktail stirrers used to hold the wick off the surface of the candle while the wax dries.

- **Wick tabs:** Used to secure wicks in container and molded candles.

Candle Success

Natural waxes need a thicker wick than that recommended for the same size candle in paraffin. When creating a drippy candle (always burned in a dish to protect floors and surfaces), use a larger wick. For a palm candle that's 2 to 2½ inches (5 to 6.4 cm) wide, try a no. 3 square braided cotton wick, and for a beeswax candle that's 2½ inches (6.4 cm) wide at its narrowest, try a no. 2 square braided cotton wick.

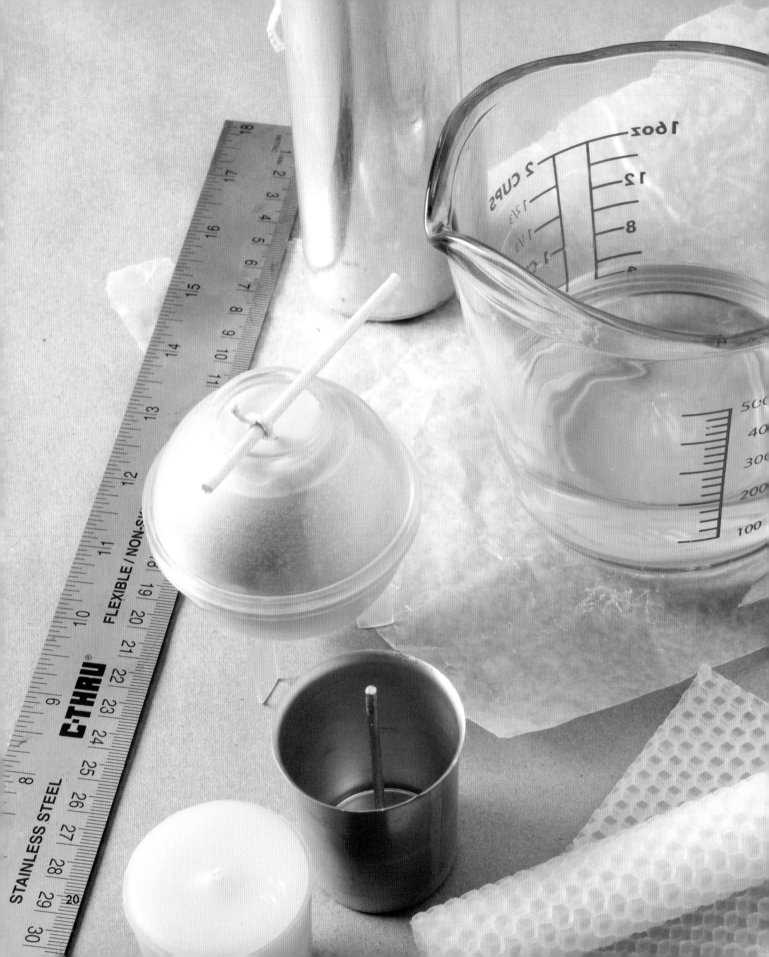

CHAPTER 2

Techniques

In this chapter you will learn the basic techniques needed to complete the projects in this book—from melting wax and adding color and fragrance to preparing molds and pouring candles. Candlemaking is not difficult, but it can be time consuming.

If you are new to the craft, consider practicing these general guidelines on test candles before attempting the candle projects. As you become more experienced, you may choose to alter the techniques to suit your candlemaking preferences, as some of the designers in this book have done.

MELTING WAX

Wax can be melted a number of ways, including in an electric slow cooker, double boiler, melting pot, or commercial wax melter. The most popular are the stove-top methods—using a double boiler or melting pot.

To begin, weigh the wax using a kitchen scale, then place the wax into the melting container. (If you are using a melting pot, place the pot in a pan of water.) Melt the wax over low-to-medium heat until it reaches the recommended melting temperature (see Melting and Pouring Temperatures chart below), also known as the melting point. The melting point is the minimum temperature that will keep wax in a liquid state. Add color and fragrance if desired (see page 23).

Once the wax cools to the recommended pouring temperature (see Melting and Pouring Temperatures chart below), pour it into the mold. Pouring temperatures are important because they affect the finished look of candles. If poured too cool, candles may mottle (a snowflake effect); if poured too hot, they may get cracks (also called jump lines). As discussed in some of the following recipes, pouring temperatures can be adjusted to achieve certain effects in finished candles.

If using a melting pot, you can pour the wax directly into the mold. If using a double boiler or electric slow cooker, you will need to transfer the wax into a pouring vessel, such as a pouring pot or heat-safe glass measuring cup. *Note:* Wipe the bottom of the melting pot or top pan of a double boiler with a kitchen towel. Doing so will prevent any water from dripping into the wax. Wear an oven glove or mitt when you do this. The wax can now be poured into a prepared container or mold.

Melting and Pouring Temperatures

Note: These are approximate temperatures; because they can vary depending on the company that makes the wax, be sure to check the manufacturer or supplier's website for specific information.

	Melting temperatures	Pouring temperatures
Beeswax	144° to 149° F (62° to 65° C)	170° F (76° C)
Palm wax	138° to 144° F (58° to 62° C)	199° to 203° F (92° to 95° C)
Soy container wax	115° to 130° F (46° to 54° C)	110° to 130° F (43° to 54° C)
Soy pillar wax	142° to 148° F (61° to 64° C)	150° to 165° F (65° to 73° C)

Candle Success

Palm wax sets very slowly and becomes cloudy and thick before solidifying by crystallizing. It's easiest to leave the candle overnight to cool completely, although it is de-moldable when the sides have pulled away from the mold and it feels only faintly warm to the touch, which takes a couple of hours. It sets from the outside in, and can look solid while being still liquid in the middle.

Palm Stearin

COLORING AND SCENTING CANDLES

If you are adding color and fragrance to your candles, you will need to heat the wax approximately 20° F (7° C) above the melting point. Check the manufacturer instructions or website for the exact temperature range for adding color and fragrance. If using liquid dye, add it to the melted wax one drop at a time; if using wax blocks, shave a small bit of the colored wax into the melted wax; if using powder dye, first mix it into a small amount of the melted wax in a separate container, then add that wax to the larger pot of wax. The most important thing you can do to ensure even distribution of color throughout your candles is to stir, stir, stir.

After adding dye, test the color by placing a small puddle of the wax on a piece of parchment paper or wax paper and let it dry. Though it won't be the exact hue of your candle, you will get a good idea of the color.

If you are adding stearin to your candle, now is the time to do it. The typical amount of stearin used is 1 to 3 tablespoons (15 to 45 ml) per pound (454 g) of wax. Be careful not to add too much; overuse of stearin can cause your candles to flake. If you are adding both stearin and dye, melt the stearin in a separate container the same way you melt wax, then add the color to the stearin and stir thoroughly. Add the colored stearin to the melted wax and stir thoroughly to incorporate the color into the wax.

After your wax is colored, add fragrance, if desired. The recommended amount of fragrance oil is 3 tablespoons (45 ml) per pound (454 g) of wax. Use more or less, depending on how strongly scented you want your candles. If you are using essential oils, add the oil drop by drop. The recommended amount of essential oil is 1 tablespoon (15 ml) per pound (454 g) of wax. Stir thoroughly to incorporate the scent into the wax. After adding color and fragrance, remove the wax from the heat.

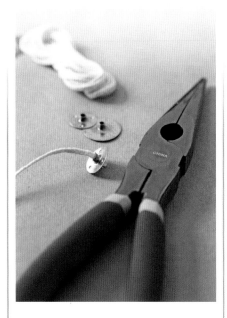

WORKING WITH WICKS

Though it is not essential, conditioning the wick before using it in a candle is advantageous. Doing so will help match the color of the wick to the finished candle and will encourage the wick to stand up straight. Conditioning the wick also makes the candle light easier and burn slower. Condition the wick by dipping it into the melted pot of wax, pull the wick taut, then lay the wick on a piece of parchment paper or wax paper to dry.

When making a container candle, or pushing a wick into a shaped candle, you will need to attach a wick tab to the wick. Thread the wick through the hole in the wick tab, then use pliers to squeeze the hole closed. Add a dab of adhesive wax to the bottom of the wick tab, then place the tab in the center of the bottom of a candle container and gently press in place, or push the wick into the premade hole of a candle.

When making a molded candle, you will need to wick the mold prior to pouring the wax. Cut a length of wick 4 inches (10.2 cm) longer than the height of the candle. If desired, condition the wick. Thread the wick through the wick hole in the mold, leaving a ½-inch (1.3 cm) tail of wick at the bottom of the mold. Secure this tail and seal the wick hole using mold sealer. Turn the mold upside down so the wick drops out of the mold. Tie the wick around a wick stick and center it on the rim of the mold. Make sure the wick is taut and straight.

After wicking the container or mold, set it on a flat surface such as a baking sheet or covered work surface. Your mold is now ready for the wax.

To ensure that your candles burn evenly and to prevent soot, trim your wick to ¼ inch (.6 cm) before and after each use.

Candle Success

Before starting any candle project, cover your work surface with newspaper. This makes cleanup easier even if you're not concerned about stains. You should also lay newspaper on the floor closest to your counter—scraping up wax drips is pure drudgery.

MAKING CONTAINER CANDLES

PREPARE THE MOLD
Using a pencil, make a light mark ¼ inch (.6 cm) below the rim of the container; this is the fill mark. Wick the container (see page 24), then place it on a covered work surface or baking sheet.

MELT THE WAX
Following the Melting and Pouring Temperatures chart (see page 22) or manufacturer's instructions, melt the wax, then add color and fragrance (see page 23). Always melt more wax than you think you'll need. You will use this wax later in the pouring process, and it is nearly impossible to create the same wax color twice.

POUR THE WAX
Following the Melting and Pouring Temperatures chart (see page 22) or manufacturer's instructions, pour the wax into the container up to the fill mark. As the wax dries, a well will form around the wick. Poke the wax around the wick with a straight pin or toothpick; this will help keep the wick centered in the mold. Re-melt the unused wax to the same temperature as you poured the candle and pour it into the well, just below the line where you poured before; this is called topping up the candle. Large candles may need to be topped up more than once.

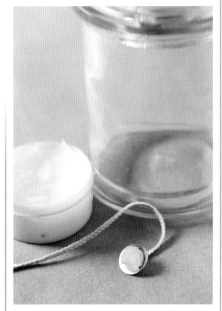

Pour any unused wax into a heat-proof glass jar. The wax can be re-melted and used in another project. Another option for saving wax is to line a bowl with parchment paper or wax paper, then pour the wax into the bowl. Once the wax has cooled, place it in a plastic bag and store for later use.

FINISH THE CANDLE
Once the candle has cooled completely, remove the wick holder and trim the wick to ¼ inch (.6 cm).

MAKING MOLDED CANDLES

PREPARE THE MOLD
Wick the mold (see page 24), then place the mold on a covered work surface or baking sheet.

MELT THE WAX
Following the Melting and Pouring Temperatures chart (see page 22) or manufacturer's directions, melt the wax, then add color and fragrance. Always melt more wax than you think you will need. You will use this wax later in the pouring process, and it is nearly impossible to create the same wax color twice. If using a melting pot, you can pour the wax directly into the mold. If using a double boiler or electric slow cooker, you will need to transfer the wax into a pouring vessel, such as a pouring pot or heat-safe glass measuring cup. *Note:* Wipe the bottom of the pouring pot or top pan of double boiler with a kitchen towel. Doing so will prevent any water from dripping into the wax. Wear an oven glove or mitt when you do this.

POUR THE WAX
Following the Melting and Pouring Temperatures chart (see page 22) or manufacturer's directions, pour the wax into the mold. As the wax dries, a well will form around the wick. Poke the wax around the wick with a straight pin or toothpick; this will help keep the wick centered in the mold. Re-melt the unused wax to the same temperature as you poured the candle and pour it into the well to just below the line where you poured before; this is called topping up the candle. Large candles may need to be topped up more than once.

Pour any unused wax into a heat-proof glass jar. The wax can be re-melted and used in another project. Another option for saving wax is to line a bowl with parchment paper or wax paper, then pour the wax into the bowl. Once the wax has cooled, place it in a plastic bag and store for later use.

Candle Success
If you don't have a double boiler you can easily create your own. Simply fill a large saucepan with water and place the melting pots inside the pan. The object is to avoid direct heat to the melting pot.

To get started, remove the mold seal. If using a metal mold, turn it upside down and tap lightly on the bottom of the mold; the candle should slide right out. If it doesn't, place the candle in the refrigerator up to 30 minutes, then try again. If you are using a two-piece plastic mold, remove the mold clips or base if necessary, then separate the pieces. Some plastic two-piece molds require that the wick be held in the mold with tape or mold sealer; for these molds, the well side will come off easily. You will need to remove the tape or mold sealer before removing the wick side of the mold.

Once the candle is out of the mold, remove the wick holder and trim the top of the wick to ¼ inch (.6 cm). Trim the bottom of the wick even with the candle. Use a paring knife to smooth any extra wax at the seams or on the bottom of the candle.

CLEANING CANDLE MOLDS

Always clean your candle mold after completing any candle project. Leftover bits of wax or dye will mar the surface of any future candle made using the mold. Be careful not to scratch or dent the mold as you clean it as these marks will also show on the surface of future candles.

To clean plastic molds, put them in the freezer for 20 minutes or so to allow the wax to contract. Gently remove the frozen wax using a toothpick (fingernails work well in a pinch), then wash the mold in a bucket of hot, soapy water. Don't wash your molds in a household sink; the wax can build up in the pipes and cause plumbing problems later on.

To clean metal molds, line a baking sheet with aluminum foil, then place the mold upside down on the sheet. Heat your oven to 200° F (93° C) then place the sheet in the oven. Leave the mold in the oven until the wax melts and runs down onto the foil. Wearing an oven mitt, remove the molds from the oven, then immediately wipe the inside of the mold using a paper towel. Wash the mold in a bucket of hot, soapy water to get out the last traces of wax.

MAKING DYE-PAINTED MOLDED CANDLES

Another technique used to create molded candles requires that the dye be painted onto the mold instead of added to the wax. This process results in candles that have interesting dye patterns on the outside of the candle (see page 52). Rebekah Ashley, one of the designers featured in this book, provided the following instructions:

PREPARE THE MOLD

Note: Metal or acrylic molds can be used with this technique.

While the wax is melting, select your color and scent (if using). To create the effect of dye on the outside of the candle, neatly apply liquid dye to the inside of the mold, either before or after wicking. You can use the blunt end of a bamboo skewer, cotton swab, or small paintbrush. Whatever applicator you choose will get stained beyond repair (unless it's metal), so you may want to avoid using expensive sable artist brushes. Wipe spills quickly with a soapy rag.

A little dye goes a long way. In a metal mold, nearly all of the wax will transfer to the candle, while in an acrylic mold, some dye is left in the mold. Also, candle dye strength varies by manufacturer. It is wise to do a test candle with plain wax and dye to play with the technique, and also to see how your chosen wick size will burn.

For the clearest results, dip the applicator, tap off the excess, and scribble or paint a design inside. It doesn't need to be too delicate—the dye is likely to drip slightly, and a blurring effect occurs as the hot wax melts the dye off the mold. The design will be clearer if the dye can dry for 30 minutes or so before pouring the wax into the mold. *Note:* Remember, most candle molds form the candle upside down, so keep this in mind when deciding where you want the design to appear on the candle.

WICK THE MOLD

Condition the wick by dipping it into the melted pot of wax, pull it taut, then lay the wick on parchment paper or wax paper to dry, then wick the mold.

POUR THE WAX

To get the best results with this technique, watch the wax as it is melting and pour it into the mold as soon as the last little bit has melted, if not a little before (a small piece of soft solid wax poured into the mold will melt anyway). Pouring the wax this cool will often cause the wax to set a little on the sides as it fills the mold, giving an interesting texture to the candle surface. If the wax gets too hot, remove it from the heat and wait until it becomes cloudy or thick looking and leaves solid wax trails in the double boiler or melting pot as you tip it from side to side.

Candle Success

It's best to let your candle cure at least a day or two before burning. Curing means to age the candle. Once a candle has hardened it looks finished, but there are still changes happening in the candle that we cannot see. Curing gives the wax and fragrance time to bond.

Remove the candle from the mold. Trim the wick close to the base with scissors or nail clippers. Then, using a sharp knife, trim the base if necessary. Trim the wick at the top to ¼ to ⅓ inch (.6 to .8 cm). If you have trouble getting the candle out of the mold, make sure it has cooled completely, then place in the refrigerator for about 30 minutes. After that, a quick rinse under a warm tap will expand the mold away from the cold candle. Then tap the mold on a counter top.

MAKING ROLLED BEESWAX CANDLES

Lay a sheet of beeswax on a self-healing cutting mat. Using a craft knife and metal-edge ruler, cut the sheet to the height of candle you wish to make. Cut a length of wick 2 inches (5.1 cm) longer than the height of the candle. Lay the wick along one end of the sheet, with 1 inch (2.5 cm) of wick past each end, then gently press the wick into the wax (see Photo A). Carefully roll over the wick end tightly once around to secure the wick (see Photo B). Continue rolling the wax until you reach the end of the sheet, then gently press the end of the sheet into the rolled candle (see Photo C). *Note:* The tighter you roll the sheet, the neater looking the finished candle. Take your time rolling the candle; you will be a pro in no time.

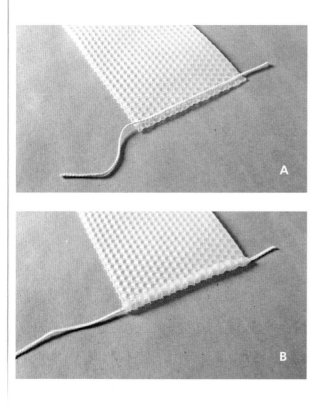

CHAPTER 3

Beeswax Candles

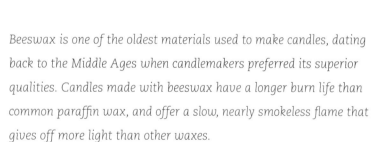

Beeswax is one of the oldest materials used to make candles, dating back to the Middle Ages when candlemakers preferred its superior qualities. Candles made with beeswax have a longer burn life than common paraffin wax, and offer a slow, nearly smokeless flame that gives off more light than other waxes.

Not only is beeswax all natural, with its own subtle honey-like scent, it's easy to mold into pillar candles or form into interesting shapes using everyday items such as cookie cutters or silicone trays. You can also roll beeswax sheets, which are available in a spectrum of colors, into beautiful candles. But don't stop there. Layer your colors and get creative with your shapes as we've done with the Mini Hearts & Stars, the Carved Rose, and the Grassy Blades candles.

Favors with Heart

CHERYL MURAKAMI

Making candles by rolling sheets of beeswax is one of the simplest
forms of candlemaking. All you need is a clean work surface,
a ruler, and a craft knife. These two-tone heart candles can be
personalized for any occasion with the colors you choose.

MATERIALS

- 1 sheet each of honeycomb beeswax: red and white or contrasting colors of your choice
- Cotton square braided wick: size 1/0, 6 inches (15.2 cm) long

TOOLS

- Craft knife
- Metal-edge ruler
- Pencil
- Self-healing cutting mat
- Wax paper

INSTRUCTIONS

1. Cut each beeswax sheet into 1 × 16-inch (2.5 × 40.6 cm) strips using the ruler, craft knife, and cutting mat.

2. For each candle you will need three strips of wax trimmed to size: one red 1 × 16 inches (2.5 × 40.6 cm); one red 1 × 8 inches (2.5 × 20.3 cm); and a contrasting color strip of white 1 × 12 inches (2.5 × 30.5 cm).

3. Cut the wick to measure 6 inches (15.2 cm) long.

4. On the cutting mat, lay the wick close to the edge of the red 1 × 16-inch (2.5 × 40.6 cm) strip with approximately ¼ inch (.6 cm) sticking out of one side (this will be the bottom of the candle). Fold the edge of the wax over the wick and press down securely. Roll the wax around the wick once tightly and evenly.

5. Lay the white contrasting color strip over the first strip starting 1 inch (2.5 cm) away from the beginning of the wick roll. Lay the last red strip over the contrasting strip starting 2 inches (5.1 cm) from the bottom strip's wick roll.

6. Carefully and slowly continue rolling the candle, incorporating the second and third strip. *Note:* Aim for an even tension roll; if it's too tight the beeswax sheet will break, and if it's too loose the roll will come apart. To finish the roll, press the seam gently into the side of the candle.

7. You can leave the round swirl design candle at this stage or continue to add another design. To make a heart shape, wrap a 2-inch (5.1 cm) length of wax paper around the pencil. Hold the candle in one hand with the seam edge toward you and, with your other hand, press the pencil into the seam to make an indentation.

8. Lay the candle on the cutting mat with the long wick side up (top of candle) and the indentation facing directly away from you. Using both hands, hold the top of the candle with your forefingers and begin pressing the bottom of the candle inward to form a "V" shape, which will be the point of the heart shape directly across the top indentation. Turn the candle over and continue shaping in the same way.

Grassy Blades

PAOLING CHE

This candle gives the look of grassy blades of beeswax filling a delightful pot. The simple project is great for beginners, and will surely brighten any room with color and life. Best part is, the plant doesn't need watering.

MATERIALS

1 sheet of green honeycomb textured beeswax: 8 × 16 inches (20.3 × 40.6 cm)

Primed wick: for candles 1 to 2 inches (2.5 to 5.1 cm) in diameter, 5 inches (12.7 cm) long

Small metal pot (pictured: 2¾-inch height × 2¼-inch [7 × 5.7 cm] base diameter)

Wick tab

TOOLS

Craft knife

Double boiler

Metal-edge ruler

Self-healing cutting mat

INSTRUCTIONS

1. Using the ruler and craft knife, score the beeswax sheet on the cutting mat, with the first cut creating a right triangle about 4 inches (10.2 cm) high with a 1-inch (2.5 cm) base.

2. Repeat the score with approximately ½ inch (1.3 cm) between each cut, parallel to the first cut. You will end up with strips of beeswax about 9 inches (22.9 cm) long. Leave the beeswax in the shape of the sheet, as you will be making additional cuts. *Note:* Working on a quarter of the sheet at a time will allow for easier management of the beeswax.

3. After finishing one diagonal direction, place your ruler up and down the length of the beeswax. Begin scoring, starting from one end of the beeswax sheet, approximately ½ inch (1.3 cm) between each cut. You should end up with long diamond-shaped beeswax pieces.

4. With the blades of grass cut into shape and size, secure the wick into the wick tab.

5. *Note:* You will create the grass shape on a covered work surface before placing it in the pot. Collect three to four longer pieces of beeswax and build them up around the wick, pressing the bottoms together to secure in place.

6. Gather pieces of beeswax blades and form four bunches of grass, about 1 inch (2.5 cm) in diameter at the base of each. Alternate direction and height to create a more natural look.

7. With the wicked piece in the middle, gather the four bunches around it and squeeze gently to secure at the base.

8. With the main part of the grass assembled, add beeswax blades to any empty spots. Test the positioning by gently dropping each into the pot to see where the bottom reaches. If it feels like the bottom doesn't touch the base of the pot, pull out the blades and condense them a bit more. If there is extra room in the pot, add more wax blades around the edges. Set aside.

9. Heat the remaining beeswax blades in a double boiler. When completely melted, pour the beeswax into the metal pot and immediately drop in the bunch of grass. This will fill any empty spots and extend the burn time of the candle.

Rolled Geometrics

CATHIE FILIAN

These easy-to-make beeswax candles are full of homemade
charm, but have a modern edge. By using cookie cutters you
will get an even shape each time. You can mix and match colors
of beeswax, or stick to a monochromatic scheme. Just keep in
mind that one color should be lighter and the other darker.

- 2 sheets of flat beeswax: one light colored, one dark colored, 17 × 8 inches (43.2 × 20.3 cm)
- Square wick raw: size 1/10

TOOLS

- Cookie cutters: circles, squares, ovals (various sizes)
- Kitchen knife
- Scissors

INSTRUCTIONS

Small Square Candles

1 Using a square cookie cutter, stamp out an even number of square shapes from one color of the beeswax. You will need at least 10 squares.

2 Cut a piece of wick that's at least ½ inch (1.3 cm) longer than the squares. Sandwich the wick in between two squares and press firmly together.

3 Evenly layer the remaining squares until you have a solid square candle. Press gently so you don't distort the beeswax pattern.

4 Using the same square cookie cutter used in step 1, stamp out two square shapes from the second color of beeswax. Using smaller cookie cutters (either circles, squares, or ovals), stamp a design into one of the squares (this will be the front of the candle). *Note:* You can mix and match cookie cutter sizes and shapes to create hundreds of different patterns.

5 Press the solid square onto the back of the candle and the stamped square onto the front of the candle. Arrange any cut pieces as desired.

Pillar Candles

1 Cut out a rectangular piece of beeswax using the kitchen knife (the longer the rectangle, the thicker the candle). The short end will be the height of the candle and the long end will be the width once the wax is rolled.

2 Cut a piece of wick that's ¾ inch (1.9 cm) longer than the height of the candle. Lay the wick across the shorter edge of the beeswax, leaving overhang on each side. Crimp the edge of the wax over the wick and roll the sheet of wax tightly and evenly.

3 Working with the second color of beeswax, cut a piece that is as tall as the rolled pillar and wide enough to wrap around the candle with a slight overhang. Using the small cookie cutters, stamp shapes out of the second color of beeswax.

4 Match one end of the second color of wax to the end of the rolled pillar. Press the ends to secure and roll. Firmly press the end of the beeswax into the candle. Trim the excess wick from the bottom of the candle.

5 To make larger candles, continue adding layers around the outside of the candle. *Note:* Over time, a film called "bloom" may appear on the surface of the candle. Heating the candle with a hair dryer can eliminate bloom; however, don't get the heat too close to the candle or you might melt the wax.

Candle Success

To create smaller shapes, try fondant icing cutters or piecrust cutters. Both can be purchased at cake decorating, general craft, and gourmet cookware shops. Also, consider adding the punched shapes by gently pressing the cut shapes onto the outer layer of the candle.

Carved Rose

PAOLING CHE

Hand molding beeswax is a fun (but sometimes a bit more difficult) way to get creative with this natural wax. Taking the time to practice this technique is the key to creating a stunning finished piece.

MATERIALS

- 2 sheets of beeswax, desired colors
- 18-gauge wire: 18 inches (45.7) long
- Primed wick: for candles 1 to 2 inches (2.5 to 5.1 cm) in diameter, 4 inches (10.2 cm) long

TOOLS

- Double boiler
- Metal baking tray
- Metal-edge ruler
- Plastic wrap
- Pliers
- Scissors

INSTRUCTIONS

Make the beeswax sheets

1 Lay the plastic wrap over the baking tray, smoothing out as many air bubbles as possible and covering the edges completely.

2 Heat one of the beeswax sheets in the double boiler until it is completely melted.

3 Pour molten beeswax into the baking tray, less than ⅛ inch (.3 cm) thick. Move the tray around to ensure even coverage.

4 Once the wax has completely cooled, lift a corner of the plastic wrap and remove from the baking tray. Peel the plastic wrap off the beeswax sheet and discard.

Assemble the rose

1 Cut one piece of beeswax approximately 2 × 4 inches (5.1 × 10.2 cm); round the corners.

2 Starting from one end on the short side, roll the piece of beeswax around the wick, pulling the top edge out as you roll and creating a petal-like look. Wrap the wax around the wick two to three times; cut off the remaining beeswax.

3 Using the scissors, cut out 10 to 15 petal shapes (like a raindrop but flat on the bottom).

4 Hold each end of the petal lengthwise and work it back and forth, stretching it slightly.

5 Attach the petals around the candle center, pressing tightly where the petals meet to secure in place. *Note:* The first inner layer holds three petals, and the second layer of petals will go between the first three.

6 Repeat steps as necessary to create the desired size and depth (about two more layers with three to five petals each).

7 Using the scissors, trim excess wax on the bottom, creating a stump that resembles the bottom of a taper candle. Make sure not to trim too high or you will disassemble the rose.

8 Adjust the height of the petals as needed, then gently press the edges of the petals with your fingers to soften the look.

Make the wired stand

1 Wrap the wire around the ruler as closely as possible, approximately 5 to 6 times; leave about ½ inch (1.3 cm) at the beginning sticking out and you should end up with about ½ inch (1.3 cm) of extra wire sticking out. Remove the ruler from the center of the wire.

2 Using the pliers, unravel the wire spiral. *Note:* You will have a zigzag-shaped piece of wire approximately 6 inches (15.2 cm) long.

3 Curl the piece around, forming a circle. Bend the ends inward like a "C" shape so they can hook onto each other.

4 Using the pliers and your hands, adjust the spacing and shape of the wire until the bottom diameter is slightly larger than the top, leaving about a 1-inch (2.5 cm) opening on top.

5 Position the rose candle into the center of the wire. The candle is now ready for use.

Mini Hearts & Stars

PAOLING CHE

Silicone ice trays make great tools when it comes to pouring your own beeswax candles. While the beeswax stubbornly sticks to other types of molds, with silicone the candle pops right out. These little heart- and star-shaped candles are perfect for gift giving.

MATERIALS

1 sheet of natural-colored honeycomb textured beeswax: 8 × 16 inches (20.3 × 40.6 cm)

4 primed wicks: for candles 1 to 2 inches (2.5 to 5.1 cm) in diameter, 1½ inches (3.8 cm) tall

TOOLS

Double boiler

Heart-shaped silicone ice tray

Metal spoon

Scissors

Star-shaped silicone ice trays

Wicking needle or votive wick pin

INSTRUCTIONS

1   Heat the beeswax sheet in the double boiler until completely melted.

2   Pour the beeswax slowly to the top of each silicone ice tray cavity, reserving about 2 oz. (60 ml) of the beeswax; set aside.

3   While the wax is still warm, insert a wicking needle or votive wick pin at the center of the wax, creating a space for the wick to be placed when the candle is cooled.

4   Once the wax has completely cooled, remove the candles from the molds by popping out the wax.

5   Poke the wax through the center again with the wicking needle to ensure there's enough room for sliding the primed wick into the candle.

6   Insert a wick into each candle, making sure the wick and candle are flush at the bottom.

7   To fill the bottom of the candles and secure the wicks in place, set the candles face down on the ice trays. Reheat the remaining beeswax in the double boiler. Using a metal spoon, scoop enough molten beeswax to fill the indent on the bottom of the candles. Let cool completely, then trim the wicks to ¼ inch (.6 cm).

Everyday Pillars

PAOLING CHE

These square pillars are perfect for the beginner candlemaker.
Beeswax sheets are available in many colors, including
white and honey-colored as pictured in this project.

MATERIALS

- 1 sheet of natural or light-colored honeycomb textured beeswax: 8 × 16 inches (20.3 × 40.6 cm)

- Primed wick: for candles 1 to 2 inches (2.5 to 5.1 cm) in diameter, 4 inches (10.2 cm) long

TOOLS

- Baking sheet
- Craft knife
- Double boiler
- Metal-edge ruler
- Plastic wrap
- Pliers
- Self-healing cutting mat

INSTRUCTIONS

1 Measure the short end of the natural beeswax sheet and mark into thirds. Using the craft knife and ruler, cut the beeswax into three long strips.

2 Lay the primed wick along the short edge of one of the natural beeswax strips.

3 Start rolling the candle by curling the edge of the beeswax over the wick (see page 29). Continue rolling tightly until the wax is about ½ inch (1.3 cm) in diameter.

4 Begin to press down instead of rolling. Turn the candle 90 degrees, pressing down again. Repeat for all four sides. You should begin forming the general shape of a square.

5 Continue the turn-and-press pattern, attaching the additional two strips of beeswax sheets to where the one before left off.

6 When all three strips have been used, press the end firmly into the candle to secure in place.

7 Heat the baking sheet in the oven until hot. Remove from the oven and place on a heat-resistant surface. Press the top of the candle down onto the baking sheet to create an even top. Lift the wick up, as it probably has been pressed into the candle. Trim the wick to ¼ inch (.6 cm).

Molded Pillar

SARA WERZEL

A beeswax pillar has a longer burn life and brighter flame than candles made from other waxes. This is a great beginner project that has endless color and embellishing opportunities.

MATERIALS

- 10 oz. (283 grams) filtered beeswax
- Medium-thick copper wire: 12 inches (30.5 cm) long
- Square braid wick: no. 2, approximately 8 inches (20.3 cm) long

TOOLS

- Candy thermometer
- Mold sealer
- Old pan: large enough to hold pouring pot
- Polyurethane candle mold: 3 × 3 inches (7.6 × 7.6 cm)
- Pouring pot
- Rubber bands
- Scissors
- Wick rod or thick wooden skewer

INSTRUCTIONS

Note: You'll need to set up your space so the mold is raised from the work surface and sits flat. I used two wooden slats placed parallel to each other, about 2 inches (5.1 cm) apart.

Melt the wax

1 Add 1 to 2 inches (2.5 to 5.1 cm) of water to the pan; bring the water to a boil.

2 Place the wax into the pouring pot and place the pot directly into the boiling water. Lower the heat to a simmer. *Note:* It is not necessary to have a rapid boil; simmering water and rapidly boiling water are the exact same temperature, 212° F (100° C).

3 Periodically add water to the pan to replace water lost to evaporation. Allow the wax to melt, monitoring the temperature until it reaches between 175° and 185° F (79° to 85° C).

Prepare the mold and pour the wax

Note: This is a two-piece mold. Use two or three rubber bands to hold the seam(s) together.

1 Form one end of the copper wire into a hook. Place the wick in the crook of the hook and feed the straight end of the wire into the hole at the bottom of the mold. Gently work the hook and wick through the hole and pull that end of the wick up through the hole, leaving the other end of the wick on the outside of the mold.

2 While keeping the wick within the wick hole, tie the opposite end of the wick to the wick rod or wooden skewer. Make sure the wick is taut and centered by pulling gently on the loose end of the wick at the bottom of the mold. Secure the wick and seal the wick hole with mold sealer.

3 When the wax has reached between 175° and 185° F (79° to 85° C), carefully pour the melted wax into the mold. Cool at room temperature for several hours.

Release the candle from the mold

1 Once the candle has cooled completely, remove the rubber bands and wick rod, then separate the mold from the candle. You may have to push the bottom of the mold to release the candle completely.

2 On the bottom of the candle, cut the wick flush with the wax. On the top of the candle, trim the wick to ¼ inch (.6 cm).

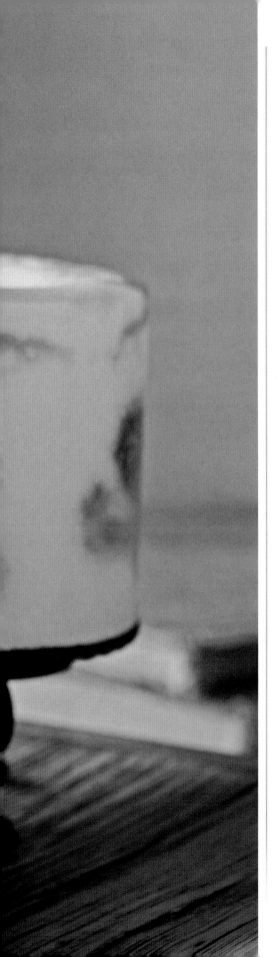

CHAPTER 4

Palm Wax Candles

Relatively new in the candlemaking arena, palm wax is an all-natural, renewable resource distilled from palm trees found in Southeast Asia, Latin America, and Africa. Palm wax makes a hard, smooth candle that is soft to the touch, and can withstand warm temperatures, absorb color easily, and retain fragrance. It is also clean burning and burns with a bright flame.

The wax also molds well, giving the candlemaker countless designs and patterns to dream up, from the crystallized hue of the Simple Molded Pillar to coordinating colors found in the Layered Pillar.

The naturally creamy color of the wax appeals to many, but if you decide to color the wax, be sure to use candle colorants. Palm wax blends well with other waxes to further expand your recipe library.

Painted Wax Pillars

REBEKAH ASHLEY

You can utilize the technique featured in this project
with any pillar candle, from 6-inch (15.2 cm), three-wick
candles to votives and tapers. I like to turn layered candles
into winter landscapes using silhouettes of trees.

MATERIALS

Liquid oil-based candle dye: dark brown, 10 to 20 drops

Pillar candle, taper, or votive

Stearin: 2 to 3 tablespoons (30 to 45 ml)

TOOLS

Aluminum foil (optional)

Art brush: desired size and shape

Mini electric slow cooker

INSTRUCTIONS

1 Place the stearin in the mini slow cooker, add the dye, and plug in the pot to heat. *Note:* If the slow cooker has a lid, I recommend putting it on to help the wax melt faster; if not, cover the pot with aluminum foil to get the same effect. Melt for 10 to 20 minutes.

2 Pick up the candle in your non-dominant hand so you can angle it and turn it conveniently as you paint it. Swish the brush around in the slow cooker to load it up with dye. *Note:* You may want to tap the brush briefly on the hot side so that the stroke doesn't start with a big drip. A little drip is fine; it will just make a thicker part of the line.

3 Create a scroll design on the candle. The wax will harden as you paint with it, so refill the brush (and remelt what's on it), by going back to the slow cooker for each stroke. Make several strokes for each scroll in the example here. You can paint over lines to widen or thicken them as you wish. You will build up a texture on very thick lines, and the crystal nature of the stearin can make interesting and unique patterns, very different and more organic than the paraffin appliqués seen in stores.

Candle Success

This embellishment technique uses stearin made from palm wax. Stearin is the best choice for this because of its high melting point compared to any other pillar wax blend. You can experiment with other waxes as long as the melting point is higher than that of the base candle. You have to work quickly, but the stearin will be hot enough to slightly melt the surface it's added to and stick well. Other waxes may be too cool when melted to fuse properly.

Dyed Sage Pillars

REBEKAH ASHLEY

An interesting effect is obtained by applying candle dye on the inside
of the mold instead of stirring it into the wax. The wax is poured
cool to prevent the stain from blending so much that it becomes
a background color. The viscosities of different wax blends and
pouring temperatures vary the amount of blurring between batches,
adding an exciting element of unpredictability to the final result.

MATERIALS

- 2 lbs. (909 g) palm wax: container blend
- Fragrance or essential oils (optional)
- Oil-based candle dye: 2 to 6 drops
- Square braided cotton wick: no. 3

TOOLS

- Baking tray with sides
- Bamboo skewers or chopsticks
- Candy thermometer
- Melting pot or double boiler
- Metal candle mold
- Metal spoon for stirring, scraping, testing, etc.
- Mold sealer
- Paring knife
- Scissors
- Soapy cloth
- White bowl: for testing the color of dyed wax

INSTRUCTIONS

1. Clip the thermometer onto the melting pot or double boiler. Melt the wax in the pot until it reaches between 199° and 203° F (92° and 95° C); remove from heat.

2. Add the fragrance oil if desired at this time and stir for 2 minutes to ensure the fragrance bonds with the wax.

3. While the wax is melting, prepare the mold by applying the dye to the inside of the mold using the blunt end of a bamboo skewer or chopstick. Wipe counter spills quickly with a soapy cloth.

4. Cut the wick 4 inches (10.2 cm) longer than the mold. Condition the wick by dipping it into the melted wax. Wick the mold and seal the wick hole with mold sealer.

5. Remove the wax from the heat; let cool to lukewarm temperature. Carefully pour the melted wax into the mold. Allow the candle to cool and fully harden.

6. Remove the candle from the mold. Trim the wick close to the base using the paring knife. Trim the wick at the top to ⅓ inch (.8 cm).

7. If you have trouble getting the candle out of the mold, make sure it's fully cooled, then place it in the refrigerator until it pulls away from the mold. Pass the mold under warm tap water to expand the mold away from the cold candle, then tap the mold on the counter.

Candle Success

Pour the candle while the wax is hot for a smoother candle surface with a more blurred design, which will start to run down toward the top of the candle. Less dye remains in the mold when the wax is hotter.

Layered Pillar

MELISSA KOTZ

My inspiration for this candle came from a beautiful
pottery pitcher. When I happened upon the glass beads
used in this project, they reminded me of the pitcher
and I decided to incorporate them into the candle.

MATERIALS

½ oz. (15 ml) fragrance oil (optional)

16 oz. (454 g) pillar blend palm wax

Beads: for the wick

Candle dye chips or liquid candle dye: brown and turquoise or desired colors

Cotton wick and wick clip

TOOLS

Candy thermometer

Melting pot or double boiler

Mold sealer (optional)

Paring knife

Pillar mold (preferably without a wick hole; if yours does have a hole, cover it with mold sealer)

Pouring pots (2)

Scissors

Wick bar or wooden skewer

Wooden spoon

INSTRUCTIONS

1 Clip the thermometer onto the melting pot or double boiler. Melt the wax in the pot until it reaches about 200° F (93° C); remove from heat.

2 Add the fragrance oil if desired at this time, and stir for 2 minutes to ensure the fragrance bonds with the wax.

3 Pour 6 oz. (180 ml) of wax into each of the pouring pots. Add dye chips or liquid dye to each pouring pot (I used brown and turquoise) and mix for at least 1 minute; repeat until the desired color is achieved.

4 Pour 1 oz. (30 ml) of the brown wax in the mold. Wait until the wax forms a thick shell but doesn't cool completely. Place the prepared wick on top of the skin, centering it with a wick bar or wooden skewer. Place the bar or skewer on top of the mold.

5 Add 1 oz. (30 ml) of the turquoise wax and wait until it forms a thick skin but doesn't cool completely. Add a thin layer of the brown wax and wait until a thick skin forms. Repeat this process, layering the two colors.

6 Carefully cut a 1-inch-deep (2.5 cm) round circle at the top of the candle with the knife, leaving about ¼ to ½-inch (.6 to 1.3 cm) sides. Gently remove the circle.

7 Pour the center with turquoise wax to refill the hole. Let candle cool completely.

8 Remove the candle from the mold. Add beads to the wick and tie a knot at the end to secure them in place. Trim the excess wick.

Candle Success

When you add the last layer of wax, wait until the top of the candle forms a thick shell. You'll want the shell to measure about 1 inch (2.5 cm) thick (the candle will still be warm). This can be a difficult thing to judge; you may want to gently poke the top of the wax with a skewer or toothpick to see how thick the shell is (kind of like checking to see if a cake is done). If liquid wax oozes out right away, wait a little longer. If very little liquid comes out, you're ready to proceed.

Simple Molded Pillar

SARA WERZEL

All-natural palm wax retains and releases great aroma using smaller amounts of fragrance oil than other waxes. The surface of a palm wax candle is uniquely patterned simply due to the nature of the wax, giving the appearance of crystalline feathers.

MATERIALS

- ¼ to ¾ oz. (15 to 22.5 ml) clove fragrance oil
- 12 oz. (340 g) palm wax
- Liquid candle dye: red, 7 drops (do not use food coloring or crayons)
- Wick: RRD 50, 8 inches (20.3 cm) long

TOOLS

- Candy thermometer
- Heat gun or blow dryer
- Long-handled metal spoon
- Metal pillar mold: 3 × 3½ inches (7.6 × 8.9 cm)
- Mold sealer
- Pan (large enough to hold pouring pot)
- Pouring pot
- Scissors
- Wick rod or thick wooden skewer

INSTRUCTIONS

Melt the wax

1 Add 1 or 2 inches (2.5 to 5.1 cm) of water to the pan; bring the water to a boil.

2 Place the wax into the pouring pot and place the pot directly into the boiling water. Lower the heat to a simmer.

3 Periodically add water to the old pot to replace water lost to evaporation. *Note:* To avoid a fire hazard, never let the double boiler run dry, and avoid splashing water into the pouring pot.

4 Melt the wax until the temperature reaches between 200° and 210° F (93° and 98° C).

Prepare the mold

1 Thread the wick through the wick hole at the bottom of the mold, leaving a ¼-inch tail of wick at the wick hole. Secure the wick and seal the wick hole with mold sealer.

2 Tie the opposite end of the wick to the wick rod or skewer, making sure the wick is centered and straight.

Candle Success

On some occasions it is obvious there is air trapped beneath the surface layer of the candle. If after about an hour of cooling you notice this, simply take a skewer and carefully poke holes in the surface of the candle. The thin surface layer can be pushed into the molten wax in the mold. This releases the air, preventing air pockets in your finished candle.

Complete the candle

1 When the wax reaches between 200° and 210° F (93° and 98° C), add the fragrance oil, then add the dye, about seven drops for a medium shade (use more for a deeper shade, less for a paler shade). Stir gently, making sure the fragrance oil and dye are incorporated. If the temperature of the wax has dropped below 200° F (93° C) by this time, place the pouring pot back into the pan with simmering water until it reaches between 200° and 210° F (93° and 98° C).

2 Using a heat gun or blow dryer, heat the mold until it is hot to the touch.

3 Carefully pour the melted wax into the mold. Let the candle cool and fully harden.

4 Once the candle has hardened, remove the mold sealer and untie the wick from the wick bar. Invert the mold and the candle will slide right out.

5 On the bottom of the candle, cut the wick flush with the wax. On the top of the candle, trim the wick to ¼ inch (.6 cm).

Candle Success

If you're using a seamless aluminum mold, you'll need to set something up so the mold is raised from the work surface and sits flat. I use two wooden slats placed parallel to each other, about 2 inches (5.1 cm) apart. Other metal molds have a base built in, making the wooden slats unnecessary.

Celestial Treasures

ANGIE RODRIGUEZ

The combination of colors and scent selected for these candles makes these not only a great gift for her, but for him as well. The cracked characteristics of the palm wax adds to its distinctive appeal.

Celestial Pillar

INSTRUCTIONS

Melt the wax

1. Clip the thermometer onto the melting pot or double boiler. Melt 1 cup (240 ml) of granule wax in the pot until it reaches about 160° F (71° C); remove from heat.

2. Using the paring knife, trim thin shavings of black wax coloring and mix them into the granule wax until desired shade is reached (use more for a deeper shade, less for a paler shade). Stir thoroughly to blend coloring evenly.

3. Add 1 to 1½ oz. (30 to 45 ml) of fragrance oil, stirring constantly to distribute evenly. When the temperature reaches 150° F (65° C), pour the wax into the cake pan; let set. Using the knife, cut various-size chunks once wax feels semi-solid.

4. While you are waiting for the chunk wax to cool, you can begin preparing the mold.

Prepare the mold

1. Thread the wick (still attached to the spool or roll; don't premeasure or cut from it yet) through the wick hole of the mold and securely tie the end at the bottom of the mold (opposite the wick hole, open end) to the wick stick.

2. Wrap the other end around the stick pin 2 to 3 times and, while holding the pin against the mold, pull tightly on the remaining wick slack to ensure the wick is taut in the mold. Once all the slack is taken up, secure with mold sealer and clip the end of the wick about ¼ inch (.6 cm) from the pin.

3. Evenly spread mold sealer to cover the exposed wick to prevent leakage when pouring.

MATERIALS

2½ to 3 oz. (75 to 90 ml) Celestial fragrance oil

3 cups (720 ml) palm pillar granule wax

Color blocks: black and royal blue

Flat braided cotton wick: 36-ply, 4 to 6 inches (10.2 to 15.2 cm) long

TOOLS

Cake pan: 9-inch (22.9 cm) round

Candy thermometer

Melting pot or double boiler

Metal round pillar mold: 3 × 3 inches (7.6 × 7.6 cm)

Mold sealer

Nail clippers

Paring knife

Straight pin

Wick stick

Pour the candle

1 Melt 2 cups (480 ml) of granule wax until the temperature reaches about 165° to 175° F (73° to 79° C); remove from heat.

2 Using the paring knife, trim thin shavings of royal blue wax coloring and mix them into the granule wax until desired shade is reached (use more for deeper shades, less for paler shades). Stir thoroughly to blend coloring evenly.

3 Once the wax reaches about 160° (71° C), add the fragrance oil, stirring thoroughly to blend.

4 Arrange chunks in the prepared mold. Pack the chunks fully for more contrast between the wax textures and colors, or sparingly for a more solid look.

5 Place the chunk-filled mold into the cake pan to trap any wax in case of leakage when pouring. Pour the wax quickly to about ¼ inch (.6 cm) from the top of the mold, reserving at least ⅛ to ¼ cup (30 to 60 ml) of wax for refilling; let set.

6 Once the candle has hardened, poke holes in various places around the wick with a straight pin; let set thoroughly before refilling.

7 Once the candle has fully solidified, reheat the reserved refill wax to 165° F (73° C). Refill the holes to cover the candle evenly. *Note:* Reheating to this temperature ensures a fairly smooth candle bottom.

8 Let set until the wax pulls away from the edges of mold. Remove the mold sealer and the candle should release smoothly.

9 Using the nail clippers, trim the excess wick at the bottom of the candle. Using the paring knife, level out the bottom of the candle, if necessary.

Candle Success

If you should experience difficulty removing the candle from the mold, place the candle in the refrigerator for 30 minutes or more, long enough for the wax to contract and the candle to pull away from the mold.

Celestial Sphere

INSTRUCTIONS

Melt the wax

1. Clip the thermometer onto the melting pot or double boiler. Melt 1 cup (240 ml) of granule wax until the temperature reaches about 160° F (71° C); remove from heat.

2. Using the paring knife, trim thin shavings of black wax coloring and mix them into the granule wax until desired shade is reached (use more for deeper shades, less for paler shades). Stir thoroughly to blend coloring evenly.

3. Add 1 to 1½ oz. (30 to 45 ml) of fragrance oil, stirring constantly to distribute evenly. When the temperature reaches 150° F (65° C), pour the wax into cake pan; let set. Cut the chunks once wax feels semi-solid.

4. While waiting for the chunk wax to cool, begin preparing the mold.

MATERIALS

2½ to 3 oz. (75 to 90 ml) of Celestial fragrance oil

3 cups (720 ml) palm pillar granule wax

Color blocks: black and royal blue

Square braided cotton wick: no. 4, 4 to 6 inches (10.2 to 15.2 cm) long

TOOLS

2-piece metal sphere/ball pillar mold and holder: 4 inches (10.2 cm)

Cake pan: 9-inch (22.9 cm) round

Candy thermometer

Medium-size binder clips (10 to 12)

Melting pot or double boiler

Mold sealer

Nail clippers

Paring knife

Rubber gasket: 4-inch (10.2 cm) diameter

Straight pin

Vegetable peeler

Wick stick

Prepare the mold

1. Place the gasket between the two halves of the ball mold. *Note:* Be certain its inner edges are aligned with the diameter of the mold and secure in place with the binder clips.

2. Thread the wick (still attached to the spool or roll; don't premeasure or cut from it yet) through the wick hole of the mold and securely tie the end at the bottom of the mold (opposite the wick hole, open end) to the wick stick.

3. Wrap the other end around the stick pin 2 to 3 times and, while holding the pin against the mold, pull tightly on the remaining wick slack to ensure the wick is taut in the mold. Once all the slack is taken up, secure with mold sealer and clip the end of the wick about ¼ inch (.6 cm) from the pin.

4. Evenly spread mold sealer to cover the exposed wick to prevent leakage when pouring.

Candle Success

This type of candle sometimes requires a little buffing when done. Use nylon stockings to massage away any shaving marks from the candle.

Pour the candle

1 Melt 2 cups (480 ml) of wax granules until the temperature reaches about 165° to 175° F (73° to 79° C); remove from heat.

2 Using the paring knife, trim thin shavings of royal blue wax coloring and mix them into the wax until the desired shade is reached (use more for deeper shades, less for paler shades). Stir thoroughly to blend coloring evenly.

3 Once the wax reaches about 160° F (71° C), add the fragrance oil and again stir thoroughly to blend evenly. *Note:* Monitor your wax temperature; you will want to pour this candle at no less than 160° F (71° C) to create the cracked characteristic of this wax.

4 Arrange the wax chunks in the prepared mold. Pack the chunks fully for more contrast between the wax textures and colors, or sparingly for a more solid look.

5 Place the chunk-filled mold into the cake pan to trap any wax in case of leakage when pouring. Pour the wax quickly to about ¼ inch (.6 cm) from the top of the mold, reserving at least ⅛ to ¼ cup (30 to 60 ml) of wax for refilling; let set.

6 Once the candle has hardened, poke holes in various places around the wick with a straight pin; let set thoroughly before refilling.

7 Once fully solidified, reheat the reserved refill wax to 165° F (73° C). Refill the holes to cover the candle evenly. *Note:* Reheating to this temperature ensures a fairly smooth candle bottom.

8 Once wax pulls away from the edges of the mold, remove mold sealer and binder clips and separate the two halves of the mold. Peel away the gasket and the candle should release smoothly.

9 Using the nail clippers, trim the excess wick at the bottom of the candle. Using the paring knife, level out the bottom of the candle. Using the vegetable peeler, shave away excess wax that built up between the gap of the two halves of the mold, if necessary.

Fresh Outdoors Pillar

ANGIE RODRIGUEZ

This candle captures the distinctive crystallization effect
of palm pillar wax. The royal blue selected for the candle
adds contrast and complements the crystallized look.

MATERIALS

½ to 3 oz. (15 to 90 ml) Fresh Outdoors fragrance oil

3 to 4 cups (720 to 960 ml) palm pillar granule wax

Color block: royal blue

Square braided cotton wick: no. 4, 6 to 8 inches (15.2 to 20.3 cm) long

TOOLS

Cake pan: 9-inch (22.9 cm) round

Candy thermometer

Melting pot or double boiler

Mold sealer

Nail clippers

Paring knife

Spiral octagon pillar mold: 4 × 6 inches (10.2 × 15.2 cm)

Straight pin

Wick stick

INSTRUCTIONS

Melt the wax

1 Clip the thermometer onto the melting pot or double boiler. Melt 1 cup (240 ml) of granule wax until the temperature reaches about 160° F (71° C); remove from heat.

2 Using the paring knife, trim thin shavings of royal blue wax coloring and mix them into the granule wax until desired shade is reached (use more for deeper shades, less for paler shades). Stir thoroughly to blend coloring evenly.

3 Add 1 to 1½ oz. (30 to 45 ml) of fragrance oil and stir constantly to distribute evenly. When the temperature reaches about 150° F (65° C), pour the wax into the cake pan; let set.

Prepare the mold

1 Thread the wick (still attached to the spool or roll; don't premeasure or cut from it yet) through the wick hole of the mold and securely tie the end at the bottom of the mold (opposite the wick hole, open end) to the wick stick.

2 Wrap the other end around the stick pin 2 to 3 times and, while holding the pin against the mold, pull tightly on the remaining wick slack to ensure the wick is taut in the mold. Once all the slack is taken up, secure with mold sealer and clip the end of the wick about ¼ inch (.6 cm) from the pin.

3 Evenly spread mold sealer to cover the exposed wick to prevent leakage when pouring.

Pour the candle

1 Clip the thermometer onto the melting pot or double boiler. Melt 3 cups (720 ml) of granule wax until the temperature reaches about 160° to 170° F (71° to 76° C); remove from heat.

2 Once the wax reaches about 165° F (73° C), add remaining fragrance oil, stirring thoroughly to blend evenly. *Note:* Monitor your wax temperature; you will want to pour this candle at no more than 160° F (71° C) to create the crystallized look.

3 Arrange the wax chunks in the prepared mold. Pack the chunks fully for more contrast between the wax textures and colors, or sparingly for a more solid look.

4 Place the chunk-filled mold into the cake pan to trap any wax in case of leakage when pouring. Pour the wax quickly to about ¼ inch (.6 cm) from the top of the mold, reserving at least ⅛ to ¼ cup (30 to 60 ml) of wax for refilling; let set.

5 Once the candle has hardened, poke holes in various places around the wick with a straight pin; let set thoroughly before refilling.

6 Once the candle has fully solidified, reheat the reserved refill wax to 170° F (76° C). Refill the holes to cover the candle evenly. *Note:* Reheating to this temperature ensures a fairly smooth candle bottom.

7 Once the wax pulls away from the edges of the mold, remove the mold sealer and the candle should release smoothly. If you have trouble getting the candle out, make sure it's fully cooled, then place in the refrigerator until it pulls away from the mold.

8 Using the nail clippers, trim the excess wick at the bottom of the candle. Using the paring knife, level out the bottom of the candle, if necessary.

Candle Success

Keep a watchful eye on the chunk wax as it solidifies. Allow it to cool long enough to harden, but not so long that it becomes fully solid. You'll want the consistency to allow cutting into strip chunks. When working with palm wax, it can be a bit tricky to judge when to cut. Palm wax tends to become brittle when cutting, so you may end up with a combination of clearly cut chunks and crumbled pieces. This is perfectly fine; each adds to the unique characteristics of the candle.

Chunky Pillar

ANGIE RODRIGUEZ

This candle is poured at a higher temperature than the
Fresh Outdoors pillar, giving the candle a rough, rustic look.
I love red, but the candle would look great in any color.
I would consider this project moderate in difficulty.

MATERIALS

- 1½ to 2 oz. (45 to 60 ml) Strawberries & Bananas fragrance oil
- 4 cups (960 ml) palm pillar granule wax
- Color blocks: red and yellow
- Square braided cotton wick: 36-ply, 6 to 8 inches (15.2 to 20.3 cm) long

TOOLS

- Cake pan: 9-inch (22.9 cm) round
- Candy thermometer
- Melting pot or double boiler
- Mold sealer
- Nail clippers
- Paring knife
- Round pillar mold: 3 x 6 inches (7.6 to 15.2 cm)
- Straight pin
- Wick stick

INSTRUCTIONS

Melt the wax

1 Clip the thermometer onto the melting pot or double boiler. Melt 1 cup (240 ml) of granule wax until the temperature reaches about 160° F (71° C); remove from heat.

2 Using the paring knife, trim thin shavings of yellow wax coloring and mix them into the granule wax until the desired shade is reached (use more for deeper shades, less for paler shades). Stir thoroughly to blend coloring evenly.

3 Add ¾ to 1 oz. (25 to 30 ml) of the fragrance oil, stirring constantly to distribute evenly. When the temperature reaches about 150° F (65° C), pour the wax into the cake pan; let set.

4 Keep a watchful eye on your chunk wax as it solidifies. Allow it to cool long enough to harden, but not so long that it becomes fully solid. Cut the wax into chunky strips. *Note:* When working with palm wax, it can be a bit tricky to judge when to cut. Palm wax tends to become brittle when cutting, so you may end up with a combination of clear-cut chunks and crumbled chunks. This is perfectly fine; it adds to the unique characteristics of each candle.

Prepare the mold

1. Thread the wick (still attached to the spool or roll; don't premeasure or cut from it yet) through the wick hole of the mold and securely tie the end at the bottom of the mold (opposite the wick hole, open end) to the wick stick.

2. Wrap the other end around the stick pin 2 to 3 times and, while holding the pin against the mold, pull tightly on the remaining wick slack to ensure the wick is taut in the mold. Once all the slack is taken up, secure with mold sealer and clip the end of the wick about ¼ inch (.6 cm) from the pin.

3. Evenly spread the mold sealer to cover the exposed wick to prevent leakage when pouring.

Pour the candle

1. Clip the thermometer onto the melting pot or double boiler. Melt 3 cups (720 ml) of granule wax until the temperature reaches about 160° to 170° F (71° to 76° C); remove from heat.

2. Using the paring knife, trim thin shavings of red wax coloring and mix them into the granule wax until the desired shade is reached (use more for deeper shades, less for paler shades). Stir thoroughly to blend coloring evenly.

3. At about 175° F (79° C), add the remaining fragrance oil, stirring thoroughly to blend evenly. *Note:* Monitor your wax temperature; you will want to pour this candle at no less than 170° F (76° C) to create the cracked look.

4   Arrange the wax chunks in the prepared mold. Pack the chunks fully for a more contrasted look between the wax textures and colors or sparingly for a more solid look.

5   Place the chunk-filled mold into the cake pan to trap any wax in case of leakage when pouring. Pour the wax quickly to about ¼ inch (.6 cm) from the top of the mold, reserving at least ⅛ to ¼ cup (30 to 60 ml) of wax for refilling; let set.

6   Once the candle has hardened, poke holes in various places around the wick with a straight pin; let set thoroughly before refilling.

7   Once the candle has fully solidified, reheat the reserved refill wax to 175° F (79° C). Refill the holes to cover the candle evenly. *Note:* Reheating to this temperature ensures a fairly smooth candle bottom.

8   Once the wax pulls away from the edges of the mold, remove the mold sealer and the candle should release smoothly. If you have trouble getting the candle out of the mold, make sure it's fully cooled, then place in the refrigerator until it pulls away from the mold.

9   Using the clippers, trim the excess wick at the bottom of the candle. Using the paring knife, level out the bottom of the candle, if necessary.

CHAPTER 5

Soy Wax Candles

In addition to palm and beeswax, soy is a popular choice with candlemakers seeking environmentally friendly materials. Soy wax is made from hydrogenated soybean oil, and it burns clean with so little smoke that it often goes unnoticed. Soy candles also emit a cleaner, stronger smell that lasts longer than paraffin, whether you're using soy wax in its natural state or adding fragrance to your candle.

Soy wax is easy to clean up with soap and water, which means you can reuse your utensils for more candlemaking and also save your work surfaces and tablecloths from wax drips and other damage.

In this chapter you'll find fun designs like the Cupcakes candles that look good enough to eat and the Seaside Memories candle, in which a seashell serves as the container.

Molded Tulip

REBECCA ITTNER

This pretty pillar lends a feminine touch to any room when displayed in a dish or on a sconce. A grouping of Molded Tulip candles in complementary colors makes a beautiful centerpiece.

MATERIALS

- ½ oz. (15 ml) rose essential oil
- 1½ lbs. (682 g) soy pillar wax flakes
- Color block: red
- Flat braided cotton wick: large

TOOLS

- Adhesive wax
- Baking sheet
- Candle thermometer
- Cellophane tape or mold sealer
- Craft knife
- Double boiler
- Glass measuring cup: 4-cup (960 ml)
- Kitchen towel
- Nylon stocking
- Paring knife
- Plastic tulip mold: two-piece with mold clips and mold stand
- Scissors
- Toothpick

INSTRUCTIONS

Prepare the mold

Note: There are two sides to this mold: the wick side and the pouring well side.

1. Cut a length of wick to fit your mold. Place one end of the wick into the indentation on the wick side of your mold and hold it in place using cellophane tape or mold sealer. Pull the wick taut and hold it in place at the opposite end using cellophane tape or mold sealer. *Note:* If you have not yet used the mold, you will need to cut the end off the pouring well. Use the craft knife to do this.

2. Press the two halves of the mold together, using the nubs in the mold to align the pieces. Seal with mold clips.

3. Using mold sealer, seal the exposed bottom and side edges to prevent the melted wax from leaking out of the mold. Using the mold base, stand the mold on a baking sheet. *Note:* You can also support the mold with an object on each side, such as heavy glasses or old books. If you are not using a mold stand, use a mold clip on the bottom edge of the mold.

Melt the wax flakes

1. Clip the thermometer onto the double boiler. Melt the wax flakes until the temperature reaches about 160° F (71° C); remove from heat.

2. Using the paring knife, trim thin shavings of red wax coloring and mix them into the wax flakes until the desired shade of pink is reached (use more for a deeper shade, less for a paler shade). Stir thoroughly to blend coloring evenly.

3. Add the essential oil, stirring constantly to distribute evenly.

Pour the candle

1. When the temperature reaches 150° F (65° C), pour the wax into the measuring cup. *Note:* Carefully wipe the bottom of the pan with a kitchen towel before pouring the wax into the measuring cup. This will prevent any water from dripping into the wax.

2. Pour the wax quickly to about ¼ inch (.6 cm) from the top of the mold, reserving at least ⅛ to ¼ cup (30 to 60 ml) of wax for refilling; let set.

3. Allow the candle to cool. As it cools, a thin skin will form on the surface of the wax (you can see this through the pour hole). Once the skin forms, poke holes in the candle near the wick using a toothpick. You will need to repeat this 2 to 3 times as the candle cools. *Note:* Cooling times vary depending on the size of your candle.

4. Once the candle has cooled completely, reheat the reserved refill wax to 160° F (71° C). Refill the holes to cover the candle evenly.

Remove the candle from the mold

1. When the candle has fully hardened, remove the mold sealer and mold clips and then gently pry the two pieces of the mold apart. *Note:* The well side of the mold will come off the wax easily. Before you can remove the wick side of the mold, remove the cellophane tape or mold sealer used to hold the wick in place.

2. Using the paring knife, trim the excess wax from the candle seams, then remove the protruding wax from the bottom of the candle where the pouring hole formed. Using the scissors, trim the bottom end of the wick.

Candle Success

If the surface of the Molded Tulip candle is uneven when removed from the mold, buff the candle with a nylon stocking to add a sheen.

Cupcakes

REBECCA ITTNER

Cupcakes are a great way to celebrate any occasion. These candles are gently scented with vanilla essential oil, but feel free to use any scent you desire or leave them unscented. Yields 6 cupcakes.

MATERIALS

- 2 teaspoons (10 ml) vanilla essential oil
- 2 lbs. (909 g) soy pillar wax flakes
- Color blocks: ivory and peach
- Flat braided cotton wick: medium
- Wick tabs: small or medium (6)

TOOLS

- Adhesive wax
- Candle thermometer
- Double boiler
- Glass measuring cups: 4-cup (960 ml) (2)
- Kitchen towel
- Metal cupcake pan
- Paper towel
- Paring knife
- Pliers
- Scissors
- Silicone baking cups (6)
- Wooden toothpicks or plastic cocktail stirrers (6)

INSTRUCTIONS

Prepare the mold

1   Thread a piece of wick through the wick tab and clamp the tab closed with the pliers. *Note:* Make sure the wick is long enough to wrap around the toothpick or stirrer at the top of the baking cup.

2   Place a dab of adhesive wax on the bottom of the wick tab, then press the tab in place in the center of the baking cup.

3   Wrap the top of the wick around the toothpick or cocktail stirrer and set it across the top of the baking cup, centering the wick in the baking cup. Place the baking cup into the cupcake pan. Repeat with the remaining baking cups. *Note:* Placing the baking cups into the cupcake pan will help hold the shape of the candles.

Melt the wax flakes

1   Clip the thermometer onto the double boiler. Melt the wax flakes until the temperature reaches about 160° F (71° C); remove from heat. Stir in the essential oil, then pour a quarter of the wax into a glass measuring cup and set it aside. *Note:* Carefully wipe the bottom of the pan with a kitchen towel before pouring the wax into the glass to prevent any water from dripping into the wax.

2   Pour the remaining wax into the second measuring cup. Using the paring knife, trim thin shavings of peach wax coloring and mix them into the remaining glass of wax until the desired shade is reached (use more for a deeper shade, less for a paler shade). Stir thoroughly to blend the coloring evenly.

Pour and finish the candles

1   Pour the wax into the baking cups, filling them about three-quarters full. Allow the wax to completely cool.

2   Once the wax has cooled, reheat the uncolored wax. You can do this by placing the measuring cup in a pan of water, then heating the water until the wax is melted. Remove the measuring glass from the pan of water. *Note:* Add water to the pan as needed.

3   Stir the wax occasionally as it cools. Once the wax begins to thicken, pour it on top of the wax in the baking cups, leaving at least ¼ inch (.6 cm) between the top of the wax and the edge of the baking cups.

4   Once the candles have completely cooled, remove the toothpicks or cocktail stirrers and, using the scissors, trim the excess wick at the top of the candles. Remove the baking cups from the cupcake pan, then remove the baking cups from the candles.

Seaside Memories

REBECCA ITTNER

Simple and quick to create, these pretty shells are perfect to use as decorations for a summer party on the patio. They also make great party favors. Bags of shells can be found at craft stores, or consider using shells found on the sand during your last visit to the shore.

MATERIALS

⅛ teaspoon (.6 ml) tea tree essential oil

½ teaspoon (2.5 ml) cedarwood essential oil

½ teaspoon (2.5 ml) eucalyptus essential oil

¼ cup (60 ml) liquid bleach

1 lb. (454 g) soy container wax flakes

Color block: blue

Flat braided cotton wick: large

Seashell: large

TOOLS

Adhesive wax

Baking sheet

Candle thermometer

Double boiler

Glass measuring cup: 4-cup (960 ml)

Kitchen towel

Mold sealer

Paring knife

Plastic bucket: 1 gallon (3.8 liters)

Pliers

Scissors

Wick tab: small

Wooden skewer

INSTRUCTIONS

Prepare the mold

1   Pour the bleach into the plastic bucket then fill the bucket with hot water. Put the shell in the water and let it sit for about 30 minutes. Carefully pour out the water and thoroughly rinse and dry the shell. *Note:* This bleach bath will disinfect the shell and remove any stains.

2   Place the shell on the baking sheet. Place a 1-inch (2.5 cm) ball of mold sealer on the bottom of the shell to make sure the shell sits evenly on the cookie sheet.

3   Thread a piece of wick through the wick tab and clamp the tab closed with the pliers. *Note:* Make sure the wick is long enough to wrap around the wooden skewer.

4   Place a dab of adhesive wax on the bottom of the wick tab, then press the tab in place in the center of the shell. Wrap the top of the wick around the wooden skewer and set it across the top of the shell, centering the wick in the container.

Melt the wax flakes

1   Clip the thermometer onto the double boiler. Melt the wax flakes until the temperature reaches about 160° F (71° C); remove from heat.

2   Using the paring knife, trim thin shavings of blue wax coloring and mix them into the wax until the desired shade is reached (use more for a deeper shade, less for a paler shade). Stir thoroughly to blend coloring evenly. Add the essential oils, stirring constantly to distribute evenly.

Pour and finish the candle

1   When the temperature reaches 150° F (65° C), pour the wax into the measuring cup. *Note:* Carefully wipe the bottom of the pan with a kitchen towel before pouring the wax into the glass to prevent any water from dripping into the wax.

2   Pour the wax into the shell, leaving about ¼ inch (.6 cm) between the wax and the edge of the shell.

3   Once the candle has completely cooled, remove the wooden skewer and trim the excess wick at the top of the candle. Remove the mold sealer from the bottom of the shell.

Tea Time

REBECCA ITTNER

These pretty candles are a great way to use orphaned teacups or mismatched sets. The candles are unscented, making them perfect for use on a dinner table (no fragrance to compete with the aromas of the food) or for allergy-prone friends. Make sure your teacup is clean and dry before starting the project.

MATERIALS

- ½ to 1 lb. (227 to 454 g) soy container wax flakes
- Color block: teal
- Flat braided cotton wick: medium
- Teacup and saucer

TOOLS

- Adhesive wax
- Candle thermometer
- Double boiler
- Glass measuring cup: 4-cup (960 ml)
- Kitchen towel
- Paper towel
- Paring knife
- Pliers
- Scissors
- Wick tab: small or medium
- Wooden skewer

INSTRUCTIONS

Prepare the mold

1. Thread a piece of wick through the wick tab and clamp the tab closed with the pliers. *Note:* Make sure the wick is long enough to wrap around the wooden skewer at the top of the teacup.

2. Place a dab of adhesive wax on the bottom of the wick tab, then press the tab in place in the center of the teacup. Wrap the top of the wick around the wooden skewer and set it across the top of the teacup, centering the wick in the container. If necessary, use a dab of adhesive wax to hold the wooden skewer in place.

Melt the wax flakes

1. Clip the thermometer onto the double boiler. Melt the wax flakes until the temperature reaches about 160° F (71° C); remove from heat.

2. Using the paring knife, trim thin shavings of teal wax coloring and mix them into the wax until the desired shade is reached (use more for a deeper shade, less for a paler shade). Stir thoroughly to blend coloring evenly.

Pour and finish the candle

1. When the temperature reaches 150° F (65° C), pour the wax into the measuring cup. *Note:* Carefully wipe the bottom of the pan with a kitchen towel before pouring the wax into the glass to prevent any water from dripping into the wax.

2. Pour the wax into the teacup, leaving about ½ inch (1.3 cm) between the wax and the top edge of the teacup.

3. Once the candle has completely cooled, remove the wooden skewer and trim the excess wick at the top of the candle. Clean the adhesive wax from the edge of the teacup with a paper towel, if necessary.

Spheres

REBECCA ITTNER

Clean, simple lines give these candles the versatility to blend in anywhere. They look great on their own or in containers. Unbuffed, the candles have a matte finish. Buffed, they have a gorgeous sheen.

MATERIALS

- 1 lb. (454 g) soy pillar wax flakes
- Color block: desired color
- Flat braided cotton wick: large

TOOLS

- Adhesive wax
- Baking sheet
- Candle thermometer
- Craft knife
- Double boiler
- Glass measuring cup: 4-cup (960 ml)
- Kitchen towel
- Mold sealer
- Nylon stocking
- Paring knife
- Polycarbonate two-piece mold: round
- Scissors
- Wooden skewer

INSTRUCTIONS

Prepare the mold

Note: There are two sides to this mold that twist together in the middle.

1. Put the two pieces of the mold together and twist to secure.

2. Cut a length of wick to fit your mold, leaving a ¼-inch (.6 cm) tail of wick at the bottom of the mold and enough length of wick at the top to wrap around the wooden skewer.

3. Using the mold sealer, cover the bottom hole and wick tail, making sure to smooth the sealer on the surface of the mold to prevent leakage.

4. Wrap the top of the wick around the wooden skewer and set in place at the top of the mold. Use a dab of adhesive wax to hold the wooden skewer in place, if necessary.

Melt the wax flakes

1. Clip the thermometer onto the double boiler. Melt the wax flakes until the temperature reaches about 160° F (71° C); remove from heat.

2. Using the paring knife, trim thin shavings of wax coloring and mix them into the wax until the desired shade is reached (use more for a deeper shade, less for a paler shade). Stir thoroughly to blend coloring evenly.

Pour the candle

1 When the temperature reaches 150° F (65° C), pour the wax into the measuring cup. *Note:* Carefully wipe the bottom of the pan with a kitchen towel before pouring the wax into the glass to prevent any water from dripping into the wax.

2 Pour the wax quickly to about ¼ inch (.6 cm) from the top of the mold, reserving at least ⅛ to ¼ cup (30 to 60 ml) of wax for refilling; let set.

3 Allow the candle to cool. As it cools, the wax may shrink away from the wick. Carefully poke holes in the wax near the wick using a toothpick. Repeat this 2 to 3 times as the candle cools. *Note:* Cooling times will vary depending on the size of your candle.

4 Once the candle has completely cooled, reheat the reserved refill wax to 160° F (71° C). Refill the holes to cover the candle evenly.

Remove the candle from the mold

1 When the candle is fully hardened, remove it from the mold. First, remove the mold sealer, then gently pry the two pieces of the mold apart.

2 Using the paring knife, trim the excess wax from the poured end of the candle. This is now the candle bottom.

3 Using the scissors, trim the ends of the wick. Buff the seams and surface of the candle smooth with a nylon stocking.

Candle Success

Candle dye is very staining and difficult to remove, especially from plastics because of the molecular similarity. It comes off wood floors well with a little bleach, linoleum with a lot (soak for hours). Sealed tiles aren't a problem but your grout could get stained beyond repair; better to put down newspaper and pick up sheets that get spilled on before they can soak through.

Bright Votives

PATRICK TROXELL

The materials needed for this project are basic and easily found at any candlemaking supply store or online source. The votives are fairly easy to make; however, it may take some trial and error before you achieve perfection.

MATERIALS

- 6 tablespoons (90 ml) fragrance oil: desired scent
- 3 lbs. (1364 g) soy pillar wax
- Liquid dye: 3 colors, 1 to 7 drops each
- Wick: small
- Wick tabs

TOOLS

- Candy thermometers (3)
- Large pan
- Melting pots (3)
- Metal spoon
- Votive molds
- Votive wick pins (optional)

INSTRUCTIONS

1 Clip a thermometer onto each melting pot and place the pots into a large pan of water. Place 1 lb. (454 g) of soy pillar wax in each melting pot.

2 Melt the wax until the temperature reaches about 165° to 170° F (73° to 76° C). Adjust the heat to a medium-low setting. *Note:* The water needs to be boiling, but it does not have to come to a rolling boil. Check the temperature of the wax occasionally to make certain it is not getting too hot. Adjust the temperature as needed.

3 While you are waiting for the wax to melt, prepare approximately 24 votive molds; add wick pins, if desired. *Note:* Ensure the molds and pins are clean by using mold cleaner or cooking spray.

4 Once the wax reaches between 165° and 170° F (73° and 76° C), add 2 tablespoons (30 ml) of fragrance oil to each 1 lb. (454 g) of wax. Add between 1 and 3 drops of dye to one of the pots and stir 3 to 5 minutes.

5 After stirring, pour the first color of wax into the molds, filling them about ¾ inch (1.9 cm), or about a third of the mold.

6 Allow the first pour to dry approximately 20 minutes at room temperature. You want the wax to harden but not dry completely or it will not fuse properly with the second and third pours. While you are waiting for the first pour to dry, maintain the second pot at about 170° to 175° F (76° to 79° C) and begin melting a third pot of wax.

7 After the first pour has dried to the desired state, ensure the second pot is at 170° to 175° F (76° to 79° C). Add 1 to 3 drops of dye and stir 3 to 5 minutes. Pour the second color of wax into the molds about another ¾ inch (1.9 cm) on top of the first pour. Allow to dry approximately 20 to 25 minutes.

8 Heat the third color of wax to between 180° and 185° F (82° and 85° C), add 1 to 3 drops of dye, and stir 3 to 5 minutes.

9 Pour the wax in the third pot to the top of the molds. *Note:* The candles will have a much better appearance if you fill the mold completely to the top.

10 Allow the candles to cool for approximately 2 hours. I do not recommend refrigerating or freezing as this could cause cracking. When the candles are completely cool they will fall right out of the molds when turned upside down. *Note:* If you are using votive wick pins, after taking the candle out of the mold, turn it upside down and lightly tap the wick pin on a flat surface. After the pin starts to come out, pull the pin completely out from the bottom of the candle.

Exotic Peach Pillars

ANGIE RODRIGUEZ

These candles are wonderfully scented with the sweet essence
of ripe peaches. The project requires a few more advanced
steps, but the stunning results are well worth the effort.

Thin Pillar

INSTRUCTIONS

Melt the wax

1. Clip the thermometer onto the melting pot or double boiler. Melt 1 cup (240 ml) of wax flakes until the temperature reaches about 160° F (71° C); remove from heat.

2. Using the paring knife, trim thin shavings of orange wax coloring and mix them into the wax until the desired shade is reached (use more for a deeper shade, less for a paler shade). Stir thoroughly to blend coloring evenly.

3. Add 1 to 1½ oz. (30 to 45 ml) of the fragrance oil, stirring constantly to distribute evenly. When the temperature reaches 150° F (65° C), pour the wax into the cake pan; let set. Using a large knife and cutting board, cut various-size chunks once the wax feels semi-solid.

4. While you are waiting for the chunk wax to cool, you can begin preparing the mold.

MATERIALS

1½ to 2 oz. (45 to 60 ml) Exotic Peach fragrance oil

3 cups (720 ml) soy pillar wax flakes

Color block: orange

Flat braided cotton wick: 24-ply, 6 to 9 inches (15.2 to 22.9 cm) long

TOOLS

Aluminum round pillar mold: 2 × 6 inches (5.1 × 15.2 cm)

Cake pan: 9-inch (22.9 cm) round

Candy thermometer

Cutting board

Knives: large and paring

Melting pot or double boiler

Mold sealer

Nail clippers

Straight pin

Wick stick

Prepare the mold

1 Thread the wick (still attached to the spool or roll; don't premeasure or cut from it yet) through the wick hole of the molds and securely tie the ends at the bottom of the mold (opposite the wick hole, open end) to the wick sticks.

2 Wrap the other end around the stick pin 2 to 3 times and, while holding the pin against the mold, pull tightly on the remaining wick slack to ensure the wick is taut in the mold. Once all the slack is taken up, secure with mold sealer and clip the end of the wick about ¼ inch (.6 cm) from the pin.

3 Evenly spread mold sealer to cover the exposed wick to prevent leakage when pouring.

Pour the candle

1 Melt 2 cups (480 ml) of wax flakes until the temperature reaches about 160° to 170° F (71° to 76° C); remove from heat.

2 Once the wax reaches about 160° F (71° C), add the fragrance oil and again stir thoroughly to blend evenly.

3 Arrange the wax chunks in the prepared mold. Pack the chunks fully for more contrast between the wax textures and colors, or sparingly for a more solid look.

4 Place the chunk-filled mold into the cake pan to trap any wax in case of leakage when pouring.

5 Pour the wax quickly to about ¼ inch (.6 cm) from the top of the mold, reserving at least ⅛ to ¼ cup (30 to 60 ml) of wax for refilling; let set. *Note:* Monitor your wax temperature; you will want to pour this candle at no more than 155° F (68° C) to prevent it from leaking.

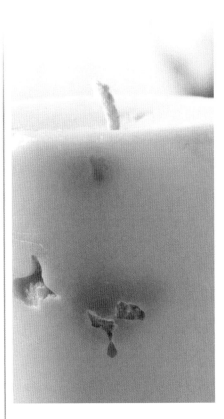

6 Once the candle has hardened, poke holes in various places around the wick with a straight pin; let set thoroughly before refilling.

7 Once the candle has fully solidified, reheat the reserved refill wax to 160° F (71° C). Refill the holes to cover the candle evenly. *Note: Reheating to this temperature ensures a fairly smooth candle bottom.*

8 Once the wax pulls away from the edges of the mold, remove the mold sealer and the candle should release smoothly. If you have trouble getting the candle out, make sure it's fully cooled, then place in the refrigerator until it pulls away from the mold.

9 Using the nail clippers, trim the excess wick at the bottom of the candle. Using the paring knife, level out the bottom of the candle, if necessary.

Thick Pillar

Melt the wax

1 Clip the thermometer onto the melting pot or double boiler. Melt 1 cup (240 ml) of wax flakes until the temperature reaches about 160° F (71° C); remove from heat.

2 Using the paring knife, trim thin shavings of orange wax coloring and mix them into the wax until the desired shade is reached (use more for a deeper shade, less for a paler shade). Stir thoroughly to blend coloring evenly.

3 Add 1 to 1½ oz. (30 to 45 ml) of fragrance oil, stirring constantly to distribute evenly. When the temperature reaches 150° F (65° C), pour into cake pan; let set. Cut the chunks once wax feels semi-solid.

4 While you are waiting for the chunk wax to cool, you can begin preparing the mold.

Prepare the mold

1 Thread the wick (still attached to the spool or roll; don't premeasure or cut from it yet) through the wick hole of the mold and securely tie the end at the bottom of the mold (opposite the wick hole, open end) to the wick stick.

2 Wrap the other end around the stick pin 2 to 3 times and, while holding the pin against the mold, pull tightly on the remaining wick slack to ensure the wick is taut in the mold. Once all the slack is taken up, secure with mold sealer and clip the end of the wick about ¼ inch (.6 cm) from the pin.

3 Evenly spread mold sealer to cover the exposed wick to prevent leakage when pouring.

MATERIALS

2½ to 3 oz. (75 to 90 ml) Exotic Peach fragrance oil

3 cups (720 ml) soy pillar wax flakes

Color blocks: orange and yellow

Flat braided cotton wick: 36-ply, 6 to 9 inches (15.2 to 22.9 cm) long

TOOLS

Cake pan: 9-inch (22.9 cm) round

Candy thermometer

Melting pot or double boiler

Metal round pillar mold: 3 × 6 inches (7.6 × 15.2 cm)

Mold sealer

Nail clippers

Paring knife

Straight pin

Wick stick

Pour the candle

1. Melt 2 cups (480 ml) of wax flakes until the temperature reaches about 160° to 170° F (71° to 76° C); remove from heat.

2. Using the paring knife, trim thin shavings of yellow wax coloring and mix them into the wax until the desired shade is reached (use more for a deeper shade, less for a paler shade). Stir thoroughly to blend coloring evenly.

3. Once the wax reaches about 160° F (71° C), add the fragrance oil and again stir thoroughly to blend evenly. *Note:* Monitor your wax temperature; you will want to pour this candle at no less than 155° F (68° C) to prevent it from leaking.

4. Arrange the wax chunks in the prepared mold. Pack the chunks fully for more contrast between the wax textures and colors, or sparingly for a more solid look.

5. Place the chunk-filled mold into the cake pan to trap any wax in case of leakage when pouring.

6. Pour the wax quickly to about ¼ inch (.6 cm) from the top of the mold, reserving at least ⅛ to ¼ cup (30 to 60 ml) of wax for refilling; let set.

7. Once the candle has hardened, poke holes in various places around the wick with a straight pin; let set thoroughly before refilling.

8. Once the candle has fully solidified reheat the reserved refill wax to 160° F (71° C). Refill the holes to cover the candle evenly. *Note:* Reheating to this temperature ensures a fairly smooth candle bottom.

9. Once the wax pulls away from the edges of the mold, remove the mold sealer and the candle should release smoothly. If you have trouble getting the candle out, make sure it's fully cooled, then place in the refrigerator until it pulls away from the mold.

10. Using the nail clippers, trim the excess wick at the bottom of the candle. Using the paring knife, level out the bottom of the candle, if necessary.

Candle Success

Candle coloring needs to be oil soluble. Water-based dyes such as food coloring are immiscible with wax; that is, they stay separated and will sink to the bottom of the melting pot if added. If you get water in your candle wax by accident, you can pour the wax into a container and let it set, then turn it out to wipe off and dry before melting anew.

Lemon Lime

REBECCA ITTNER

This bright citrus candle is a great addition to any kitchen or bathroom. For a personalized hostess gift, make the candle in colors that complement the recipient's home. Create a dramatically lit setting by placing multiple container candles on surfaces throughout a room—perfect for a romantic dinner.

MATERIALS

- 1 teaspoon (5 ml) lemon essential oil
- 1 teaspoon (5 ml) lime essential oil
- 1½ lbs. (681 g) soy container wax flakes
- Color blocks: avocado and yellow
- Flat braided cotton wick: large
- Glass container with lid: large

TOOLS

- Adhesive wax
- Candle thermometer
- Double boiler
- Glass measuring cups: 4-cup (960 ml) (2)
- Kitchen towel
- Paring knife
- Pliers
- Scissors
- Wick tab: small or medium
- Wooden skewer

INSTRUCTIONS

Prepare the mold

1. Thread a piece of wick through the wick tab and clamp the tab closed with the pliers. *Note:* Make sure the wick is long enough to wrap around the wooden skewer.

2. Place a dab of adhesive wax on the bottom of the wick tab, then press the tab in place in the center of the glass jar.

3. Wrap the top of the wick around the wooden skewer and set it across the top of the glass jar, centering the wick in the jar. Hold the wooden skewer in place with a dab of adhesive wax, if necessary.

Melt the wax flakes

1. Clip the thermometer onto the double boiler. Melt the wax flakes until the temperature reaches about 160° F (71° C); remove from heat.

2. Pour half of the melted wax into each measuring cup. *Note:* Carefully wipe the bottom of the pan with a kitchen towel before pouring the wax into the glass to prevent any water from dripping into the wax.

3. Using the paring knife, trim thin shavings of avocado wax coloring into one measuring cup and mix them in with with the wax until desired shade is reached (use more for a deeper shade, less for a paler shade). Stir thoroughly to blend coloring evenly. Add the lime essential oil, stirring constantly to distribute evenly.

4. Repeat with the yellow wax and lemon essential oil in the second measuring cup of melted wax.

Pour and finish the candle

1   When the temperature reaches 130° F (54° C), pour a layer of avocado wax into the mold and let it harden.

2   Once the wax has hardened, pour a layer of yellow wax on top of the avocado wax and let it harden. *Note:* You will need to reheat the wax to 130° F (54° C) to pour the layers.

3   Repeat to fill the container, leaving about 1 inch (2.5 cm) between the wax and the top of the container (this will allow room for the lid of the jar).

4   Once the candle has completely cooled, remove the wooden skewer and trim the excess wick at the top of the candle.

Candle Success

If using dye chips, you can add one or two chips to the wax and mix to test the color. Test your shades on a white plastic lid from a discarded yogurt or margarine container. Carefully pour a spoonful of melted wax on the lid. It usually takes about five minutes or so to harden completely, revealing its true color. You can do the same for liquid dye, but keep in mind that most liquid dyes are in concentrated form and will result in a much darker shade. Dip the very tip of a wooden skewer in the liquid dye tube and mix the dye into the hot wax with the wooden skewer. This gives you complete control over the shade.

Fluted Pillar

ANGIE RODRIGUEZ

A combination of simple instructions and natural ingredients is the key to creating this soy candle. I've added no coloring; the variations in the shading come from the fragrance oils and the wax's natural beige tones. This project is great for beginner candle crafters. The following instructions are for one candle.

MATERIALS

- 1½ to 2 oz. (45 to 60 ml) White Peach Hibiscus fragrance oil

- 2½ cups (567 g) soy pillar wax flakes

- Flat braided cotton wick: 24-ply, 6 to 9 inches (15.2 to 22.9 cm) long

TOOLS

- Cake pan: 9-inch (22.9 cm), round

- Candy thermometer

- Melting pot or double boiler

- Mold sealer

- Nail clippers

- Paring knife

- Round or oval spiral fluted pillar mold: 3 × 6 inches (7.6 × 15.2 cm)

- Straight pin

- Wick stick

INSTRUCTIONS

Prepare the mold

1 Thread the wick (still attached to the spool or roll; don't premeasure or cut from it yet) through the wick hole of the mold and securely tie the end at the bottom of the mold (opposite the wick hole, open end) to the wick stick.

2 Wrap the other end around the stick pin 2 to 3 times and, while holding the pin against the mold, pull tightly on the remaining wick slack to ensure the wick is taut in the mold. Once all the slack is taken up, secure with mold sealer and clip the end of the wick about ¼ inch (.6 cm) from the pin.

3 Evenly spread mold sealer to cover the exposed wick to prevent leakage when pouring.

Pour the candle

1   Clip the thermometer onto the melting pot or double boiler. Melt the wax flakes in the pot until the temperature reaches about 160° to 170° F (71° to 76° C); remove from heat.

2   Once the wax reaches about 160° F (71° C), add fragrance oil and stir thoroughly to blend evenly.

3   Place the prepared mold into the cake pan to trap any wax in case of leakage when pouring. Pour the wax quickly to about ¼ inch (.6 cm) from the top of the mold, reserving at least ⅛ to ¼ cup (30 to 60 ml) of wax for refilling; let set. *Note:* Monitor your wax temperature; you will want to pour this candle at no more than 150° F (65° C) to prevent it from leaking.

4   Once the candle has hardened, poke holes in various places around the wick with a straight pin; let set thoroughly before refilling.

5   Once the candle has fully solidified, reheat reserved refill wax to 160° F (71° C). Refill the holes to cover the candle evenly. *Note:* Reheating to this temperature ensures a fairly smooth candle bottom.

6   Once the wax pulls away from the edges of the mold, remove the mold sealer and the candle should release smoothly. If you have trouble getting the candle out, make sure it's fully cooled, then place in the refrigerator until it pulls away from the mold.

7   Using the nail clippers, trim the excess wick at the bottom of the candle. Using the paring knife, level out the bottom of the candle, if necessary.

CHAPTER 6

Upcycled Candles

Whether you have a stash of nearly spent candles, or a couple of candle projects that didn't turn out so well, there's no reason to waste the unwanted. The beauty of candle wax is that it can be reheated and melted at any state, combined with other waxes, and recolored and remade into a beautiful new candle.

In this chapter you'll find a project that camouflages a dented candle with tissue paper, candles that have been melted and poured into new molds and containers, and candles completely made over by embedding fresh wax and embellishments.

You can also upcycle candles that are faded, stained, or simply outdated in color or style.

Tissue Paper Transfers

CATHIE FILIAN

With a few stamping supplies, tissue paper, and a little creativity you can transform a plain pillar into a boutique-style candle in a matter of minutes. The technique is so easy and the results are stunning.

MATERIALS

Embossing inkpad or dark ink

Embossing powder

Light-colored pillar candle: desired size

Parchment paper

Watercolor paint

White tissue paper

TOOLS

Embossing gun

Manila file folder

Paintbrush

Rubber stamp

Scissors

INSTRUCTIONS

1 Cut a piece of white tissue paper that is large enough for the rubber stamp.

2 Ink the stamp onto the glossy side of the tissue paper. If you're using a larger stamp, place the inked stamp rubber-side up on the work surface, lay the tissue paper on top of the stamp, and gently rub the paper to fully transfer the image. Gently lift the tissue paper from the stamp.

3 Sprinkle embossing powder on the inked image and tap off the excess, working over a manila file folder. When finished, funnel excess embossing powder back into its jar.

4 Using an embossing gun, heat the powder onto the candle until the image is embossed.

5 Swirl a wet paintbrush in the watercolor paint and color in the background of the stamp; allow to dry about 10 to 20 minutes. *Note:* Make sure your paintbrush is not too wet or your tissue paper may tear.

6 Cut a piece of parchment paper large enough to cover the image and wrap around the candle, plus an extra 2 inches (5.1 cm) of length.

7 Trim the excess tissue paper around the edges of the image, then place the image on the surface of the candle. *Note:* The embossed side of the image can face in toward the candle or outward, depending on your preference.

8 Wrap the parchment paper tightly around the candle, using the excess parchment paper in the back as a handle.

9 Moving the embossing gun over the image, melt the tissue paper into the candle. Once you see wax melt through the parchment paper in one area, move the embossing gun to another area so as not to melt the candle too much. When the entire image has melted into the candle, carefully remove the parchment paper.

Chunky Pyramid

REBECCA ITTNER

While making a layered pillar candle, I didn't wait long enough between pouring the layers. The result was a really ugly colored candle. Instead of throwing it away, I cut the candle into medium-sized pieces and used them to make this chunky layered candle. The original pillar candle was heavily scented, so no additional scent was used.

MATERIALS

- 3 lbs. (1364 g) soy pillar wax
- Flat braided cotton wick: extra large
- Pillar candle: 3 × 9 inches (7.6 × 22.9 cm), desired color
- Vegetable spray

TOOLS

- Baking sheet
- Candle thermometer
- Double boiler
- Glass measuring cup: 4-cup (960 ml)
- Kitchen towel
- Knives: large and paring
- Metal pyramid mold with base
- Mold sealer
- Scissors
- Wooden skewer

INSTRUCTIONS

Note: Before preparing the mold, cut the colored pillar candle into medium- and large-size chunks. Use the paring knife to smooth any rough edges.

Prepare the mold

1. Cut a length of wick 3 inches (7.6 cm) longer than the height of the mold, then thread one end of the wick through the wick hole. Cover the top of the wick and the wick hole with mold sealer.

2. Spray the inside of the mold with vegetable spray, then place the mold upside down into the mold base on the baking sheet.

Melt the wax flakes and pour the candle

1. Clip the thermometer onto the double boiler. Melt the wax until the temperature reaches about 160° F (71° C).

2. When the temperature reaches 160° F (71° C), pour the wax into the measuring cup. *Note:* Carefully wipe the bottom of the double boiler with a kitchen towel before pouring the wax into the mold. This will prevent any water from dripping into the wax.

3. When the temperature reaches about 130° F (54° C), pour a thin layer of wax into the mold, about 1 inch (2.5 cm) thick. Let the wax cool.

4. Arrange a layer of candle chunks on top of the wax, then pour a layer of wax over the chunks until the wax just covers the chunks. Let the wax cool.

5. Repeat this layering-and-pouring process until the mold is filled and there is an even layer of wax at the top of the mold. Let the candle cool completely. *Note:* Reheat the wax as necessary to complete the candle; however, make sure to pour the wax when it is no hotter than 130° F (54° C) to prevent the wax chunks from melting and the wax from leaking from the mold.

Finish the candle

1. Remove the mold sealer then turn the mold upside down. If the candle doesn't slide out easily, set the mold back in the base and then place the mold in a refrigerator for a few minutes and try again.

2. Once the candle has been removed from the mold, trim the wick with the scissors.

Travel Mates

REBECCA ITTNER

Leftover, nearly gone container candles were used to create these clever travel candles. This is a great project because you get to use wax that might otherwise be thrown away.

MATERIALS

Flat braided cotton wick: medium

Partially used soy container candles

Wick tab: small

TOOLS

Adhesive wax

Aluminum container with lid

Craft scissors

Kitchen towel

Metal spoon

Oven mitt or glove

Pliers

Saucepan

Wooden skewer

INSTRUCTIONS

Prepare the mold

1 Thread a piece of wick through the wick tab and clamp the tab closed with the pliers. *Note:* Make sure the wick is long enough to wrap around the wooden skewer.

2 Place a dab of adhesive wax on the bottom of the wick tab, then press the tab in place in the center of the aluminum container.

3 Wrap the top of the wick around the wooden skewer and set it across the top of the container, centering the wick in the container. Hold the wooden skewer in place with a dab of adhesive wax if necessary.

Melt the wax flakes

1 Place the container into a saucepan of water about 2 inches (5 cm) deep and let the water simmer on medium-to-low heat until the wax is melted.

2 Wearing an oven mitt or glove, remove the jar from the water, then wipe the bottom of the jar with a kitchen towel to remove any water drops. Using the metal spoon, carefully remove any old wick or wick tab.

Pour and finish the candle

1 Pour the wax into the aluminum container, leaving about ½ inch (1.3 cm) between the top of the wax and the edge of the container. Allow the wax to harden.

2 Once the candle has completely cooled, remove the wooden skewer and trim the excess wick at the top of the candle.

Floating Lights

REBECCA ITTNER

I used wax that was left over from the Tea Time candle to create these pretty flowers. Palm stearin was added to the melted wax to harden it for use as a floating candle. To create an easy centerpiece, place a handful of the floating candles in a bowl of water, then light the wicks. Yields 6 to 8 floating candles.

MATERIALS

- 1 lb. (454 g) soy container or pillar wax, left over from previous projects
- Flat braided cotton wicks: small (6–8)
- Palm stearin (if using container wax)

TOOLS

- Adhesive wax
- Candle thermometer
- Double boiler
- Glass measuring cup: 4-cup (960 ml)
- Kitchen towel
- Metal floating candle molds: small (6–8)
- Pliers
- Scissors
- Wick tabs: small (6–8)
- Wooden toothpicks or plastic cocktail stirrers

INSTRUCTIONS

Prepare the molds

1 Thread a piece of wick through the wick tab and clamp the tab closed with the pliers. *Note:* Make sure the wick is long enough to wrap around the toothpick or cocktail stirrer.

2 Place a dab of adhesive wax on the bottom of the wick tab, then press the tab in place in the center of the mold. Wrap the top of the wick around the toothpick or cocktail stirrer and set it across the top of the mold. Hold it in place with a dab of adhesive wax, if necessary.

3 Repeat steps 1 and 2 to prepare each mold.

Melt the wax flakes

Note: Stearin is added to container wax at a rate of 1 to 3 tablespoons (15 to 45 ml) per 1 lb. (454 g) of wax to harden it and increase burn time. I added 1 tablespoon (15 ml) to each ½ lb. (226 g) of colored wax. You do not need to add the stearin if you are using leftover pillar wax.

1 Clip the thermometer onto the double boiler. Melt the wax until the temperature reaches about 160° F (71° C); add the stearin and stir until it melts into the wax.

2 Remove the pan from the heat then pour the melted wax into a measuring cup. *Note:* Carefully wipe the bottom of the pan with a kitchen towel before pouring the wax into the glass. This will prevent any water from dripping into the wax.

Pour and finish the candles

1 When the temperature reaches 150° F (65° C), pour the wax into the molds and allow it to harden.

2 Once the candles have completely cooled, remove them from the molds. Remove the toothpicks or cocktail stirrers and, using the scissors, trim the excess wick at the top of the candles.

Embedded Pillars

REBECCA ITTNER

I used coffee beans to create these candles, but dried flowers or chunks of colored wax would work well too.

MATERIALS

- 1 lb. (454 g) soy pillar wax
- 1 lb. (454 g) whole coffee beans
- Flat braided cotton wick: large
- Vegetable spray
- White pillar candle: 3 × 6 inches (7.6 × 15.2 cm)

TOOLS

- Baking sheet
- Candle thermometer
- Double boiler
- Glass measuring cup: 4-cup (960 ml)
- Kitchen towel
- Metal pillar mold with base
- Mold sealer
- Scissors
- Wooden chopstick

INSTRUCTIONS

Prepare the mold

1 Cover the bottom of the wick hole with mold sealer.

2 Spray the inside of the mold with vegetable spray, then place the pillar candle in the center of the mold; set aside.

Melt the wax

1 Clip the thermometer onto the double boiler. Melt the pillar wax until the temperature reaches about 160° F (71° C); let cool.

2 When the temperature reaches 130° F (54° C), pour the wax into the measuring cup. *Note:* Carefully wipe the bottom of the double boiler with a kitchen towel before pouring the wax to prevent any water from dripping into the wax.

Pour and finish the candle

1 Pour a thin layer of wax about ¼ inch (.6 cm) thick into the mold on the outside of the pillar, taking care to avoid pouring wax on the top of the candle; let cool.

2 Pour a layer of coffee beans onto the cooled wax then pour some more wax on top of the coffee beans.

3 Using the wooden chopstick, evenly distribute the beans around the candle. Let the wax cool. *Note:* The coffee beans will float so it is important that just enough wax is poured to cover them.

4 Repeat this layering-and-pouring process until the coffee beans are even with the top of the candle. *Note:* Reheat the wax as necessary to complete the candle. If the top of the candle is marred, cover it with a thin layer of wax; just make sure that the wax doesn't bury the wick.

5 Once the candle has completely cooled, remove the mold sealer, then turn the mold upside down to remove the candle. If the candle doesn't slide out easily, place the mold in a refrigerator for a few minutes then try again.

Natural Beauty

REBECCA ITTNER

Quickly transform plain, ho-hum pillars using this simple
dipping method. Thin objects such as reeds, dried flowers, or
photographs work best. Uncolored wax provides the clearest view
of the embedded items, but colored wax would also work.

MATERIALS

1½ to 2 lbs. (685 to 908 g) soy container wax flakes

Dried reeds

Small pillar or votive candle

Stearin: 5 tablespoons (75 ml)

TOOLS

Candle thermometers (2)

Double boilers (2)

Newspaper

Parchment paper

Pouring pot or tall, thin jar

Scissors

INSTRUCTIONS

Prepare the reeds

Measure the height of the candle and cut the desired amount of reeds the same height or a bit shorter than the candle. Set aside.

Melt the wax

Note: Melt the palm stearin and soy wax flakes in separate containers at the same time. You will need to add the palm stearin to the wax once both reach their melting points.

1. Clip a thermometer onto a double boiler. Melt the palm stearin until the temperature reaches about 135° F (57° C).

2. Clip a thermometer onto the remaining double boiler. Melt the soy wax flakes until the temperature reaches about 125° F (52° C); remove from heat, then stir in the palm stearin. Let the wax cool to about 110° F (43° C), then pour it into the pouring pot or jar.

Dip the candle

1. Pick up the candle by the wick and carefully dip the candle into the melted wax. Lift the candle out of the wax, then let the excess wax drip back into the melted wax. Set the candle onto the parchment paper.

2. Working quickly, carefully press the cut pieces of reed into the wax. Allow the wax to cool.

3. Once the candle has cooled, reheat the wax, then let it cool to about 110° F (43° C). Repeat Step 1.

4. Once the candle has completely cooled, use the paring knife to trim any excess wax from the bottom edge of the candle, if desired.

Cookie Cutter Shapes

REBECCA ITTNER

These layered candles are the result of a damaged beeswax pillar.
I remelted the failed candle, then poured the wax into a cake
pan and used cookie cutters to cut shapes in the warm wax.

MATERIALS

- 2 lbs. (909 g) flat beeswax: 2 coordinating colors
- Flat braided cotton wicks: large (3)
- Vegetable spray
- Wick tabs: small (3)

TOOLS

- Cake pans: 9-inch (22.9 cm) round (2)
- Candle thermometer
- Cookie cutters: various shapes and sizes
- Double boiler
- Kitchen towel
- Parchment paper
- Pliers
- Scissors
- Tongs
- Votive wick pin

INSTRUCTIONS

1 Cover your work surface with parchment paper. Spray the cake pans with vegetable spray; set aside.

2 Clip the thermometer onto the double boiler. Melt one color of the wax until the temperature reaches about 160° F (71° C).

3 Cut a 12-inch (30.5 cm) length of wick. Using the tongs, dip the wick into the melted wax twice. Pull the wick taut, then set the dipped wick on the parchment paper to dry.

4 When the temperature reaches 160° F (71° C), pour the wax into one of the cake pans. *Note:* Carefully wipe the bottom of the double boiler with a kitchen towel before pouring the wax into the cake pan to prevent any water from dripping into the wax.

5 Repeat steps 1 to 4 with the second color of wax.

6 Let the wax cool to the point where it is rubbery. Using the cookie cutters, cut shapes from the wax and place the shapes on the flat, parchment paper-covered surface; let cool. *Note:* You may need to use pliers to remove the cookie cutter from the wax.

7 Stack the shapes in alternating colors, then push the votive wick pin through the center of the stacked shapes.

8 Cut a length of wick 2 inches (5.1 cm) longer than the height of the stacked shapes, thread the wick through a wick pin, and close the wick pin with the pliers. Thread the wick up through the stack of shapes. *Note:* If the wick gets too soft to thread through the shapes, put it in the freezer for a few minutes and try again.

Candle Success

Keep an eye on the cake pans as the wax is cooling. You will need to use the cookie cutters when the wax is warm and rubbery, not liquid. If the wax cools too much, the cookie cutters will not go through the wax.

Wax Rejects

REBECCA ITTNER

Every candle maker has a stash of leftover wax in various
colors. When there's not enough wax in any one color
or coordinating colors to create a pretty candle, consider
melting them all together and pouring them in an interesting
porcelain or metal container to conceal the mottled color.

- 1 to 1½ lbs. (454 to 681 g) leftover colored soy container wax
- Flat braided cotton wick: large

TOOLS

- Adhesive wax
- Candle thermometer
- Container: porcelain or metal
- Double boiler
- Glass measuring cup: 4-cup (960 ml)
- Kitchen towel
- Paper towel
- Pliers
- Scissors
- Wick tab: medium
- Wooden skewer

INSTRUCTIONS

Prepare the mold

1 Thread a piece of wick through the wick tab and clamp the tab closed with the pliers. *Note:* Make sure the wick is long enough to wrap around the wooden skewer at the top of the container.

2 Place a dab of adhesive wax on the bottom of the wick tab, then press the tab in place in the center of the container. Wrap the top of the wick around the wooden skewer and set it across the top of the container, centering the wick in the container. If necessary, use a dab of adhesive wax to hold the wooden skewer in place.

Melt and pour the candle

1 Clip the thermometer onto the double boiler. Melt the colored wax until the temperature reaches about 160° F (71° C); remove from heat.

2 When the temperature reaches 150° F (65° C), pour the wax into the measuring cup. *Note:* Carefully wipe the bottom of the pan with a kitchen towel before pouring the wax into the glass. This will prevent any water from dripping into the wax.

3 Pour the wax into the container, leaving about ¼ to ½ inch (.6 cm to 1.3 cm) between the wax and the top edge of the container.

Finish the candle

1 Once the candle has completely cooled, remove the wooden skewer and trim the excess wick at the top of the candle.

2 Clean the adhesive wax from the edge of the container with a paper towel, if necessary.

MEET THE DESIGNERS

Rebekah Ashley

Rebekah Ashley has been making candles since she was a teenager. Growing up in Boscastle, Cornwall, the British-born visual artist remembers a wonderful little candle shop set in an ancient stone cottage. Multi-colored candles scented with lavender, jasmine, and sandalwood were displayed, and upstairs in the tiny attic, a workshop was open to demonstrations. Soon after she discovered the shop, Rebekah was given a regular craft store candlemaking kit as a gift, and she's been making candles ever since.

Rebekah likes to change what she's doing often and her work reflects this with her many eclectic crafts and art objects, from jewelry and candles to hand-painted ornaments and wall art.

Check out Rebekah's work at www.ashleygrove.com.

Paoling Che

Paoling Che is an extraordinary girl in an often ordinary world. Although she is also a graphic designer and artist, candlemaking is one of Paoling's main outlets for creative expression. Inspired by daydreaming and the moments between real life, her goal is to create something that's a tiny bit amusing and a big bit different.

Check out Paoling's work at www.paolingche.com or www.kokocandles.com.

Cathie Filian

Cathie Filian brings a fresh approach to creative living with her outside-the-box ideas for crafts, recipes, and home décor. Cathie is an Emmy-nominated television host, book author, columnist, lifestyle expert, and designer. She created, produced, and co-hosted the HGTV and DIY lifestyle shows *Creative Juice* and *Witch Crafts*. Cathie has also appeared on Discovery Channel, HGTV, DIY, and Food Network and authored *101 Snappy Fashions* (Lark Books, 2010), *Bow Wow WOW!* (Lark Books, 2008), and *Creative Juice: 45 Re-Crafting Projects to Make with Recycled Stuff*.

Cathie lives in Los Angeles with her husband, Eddie, and their dog, Max.

Check out Cathie's work at www.cathiefilian.com.

Melissa Kotz

The candles of Melissa Kotz, owner of Arte de Cera Candles, are unlike any candle you'll find in stores. Melissa uses inventive techniques to meticulously and beautifully hand craft her candles. Each masterpiece is not just a candle but a true work of art.

Her designs include hand-carved and sculpted candles, which resemble pottery bowls, unique pillars, and votives, and many other designs and styles. She uses only eco-friendly biodegradable waxes such as soy and palm. Most of her candles are embellished with beautiful beads, used to decorate the wicks of her candles.

Check out Melissa's work at www.artedecera.etsy.com or www.theartofwax.weebly.com.

Cheryl Murakami

Cheryl Murakami has always loved art and creating things with her hands. Years ago, she married a fellow artist and, to support themselves, they started a candlemaking business in 1996 with one inspired idea. That now-famous design was for hand-rolled beeswax sushi candles.

Since then, with the ever-increasing appreciation for sushi candles, Cheryl has been working on a book about how to make a variety of sushi candles to share her knowledge with other crafters and lovers of sushi.

Check out Cheryl's work at www.doublebrush.com.

Angie Rodriguez

Angie Rodriguez, proprietor of Crafty Hands Candles, began candlemaking one holiday season long ago to create unique gifts for family. After some kooky-looking results and lots of laughs, determination and an artistic intrigue set in. She grew to love candle experimenting and eventually candlemaking, particularly pillar candles. "Free-standing pillar candles hold their own character to me," she says.

Throughout the years, Angie has discovered various ways of making her hand-poured candles unique. Today, Angie sells her Crafty Hands Candles online. Her candles can also be found at East End Urban Market in Houston, Texas.

Check out Angie's work at www.craftyhandscandles.etsy.com.

Patrick Troxell

A well-traveled Patrick Troxell looked into candlemaking to save money—and to make a little, too. The U.S. Marine had watched his girlfriend buy candle after candle, and he thought they couldn't be that difficult to make. After a few batches of burned wax and some tinkering here and there with color and fragrances, Patrick now crafts beautiful candles in all shapes and sizes, including two- and three-layer soy candles, birthday candles, and scented votives.

Check out Patrick's work at www.sagewick.etsy.com.

Sara Werzel

Sara Werzel, owner and operator of Auntie B's Wax, has been pouring candles for more than a decade. When she isn't in the studio wallowing in the rich aromas of fragrance oils and answering to the name Bee Head, Sara is pushing papers for the State of Minnesota.

Check out Sara's work at www.auntiebonline.etsy.com.

ABOUT THE AUTHOR

Rebecca Ittner was raised in California in a family where creativity was encouraged. Instead of staying inside watching television, she and her siblings played with clay, drew, painted with watercolors (or at least tried to), and, in general, made their own fun.

She is now a magazine and book editor, writer, photo stylist, and craft enthusiast. She says, "It took me a long time to figure out that I could do what I love and make a living at it. I am incredibly blessed." Rebecca's work has been featured in *Romantic Homes, Somerset Studio Take Ten, Somerset Home,* and *Somerset Life* magazines and many craft books. She also appeared on The Christopher Lowell Show.

To see more of Rebecca's work, visit www.rebeccaittner.etsy.com or read her blog at www.livelovecraft.com.

ACKNOWLEDGMENTS

Thank you to my loving and supportive family. Mom, you are my hero; I am honored to be your daughter. Your courage, strength, and unwavering love are the best gifts a mother could give. Your thirst for knowledge, boundless curiosity, and ability to rise to any challenge with grace and dignity fill me with love, admiration, and gratitude. It was you who fanned my creative flame and supported my artistic endeavors. Your love and example will inspire me always.

Debbie, Pete, and Perry, I am thankful for you every day. There is nothing more precious than family, and I am lucky you are mine. Debbie, you manage to squeeze more into one day than anyone I know. You are the best big sister and friend. I love making up for lost time! Pete, thank you for your kindness, love, wisdom, and for always taking care of the details. Perry, you have been my best friend my whole life. Thank you for your support and understanding, and for always knowing how to crack me up.

Thank you to Peter, my rock and my soft place to land. You make my life beautiful. Who knew magic happens at airports? Life is so much sweeter with you by my side and I am grateful for you every day. Only you could be so supportive, patient, and kind while I turned the kitchen into a craft workshop.

I am deeply indebted to the amazing group of women at Red Lips 4 Courage. Eileen, I am grateful for the experiences we have shared through the years, and I cherish your friendship. Cathy, thank you for your support, time, and editing prowess over the surprising course of this book. You, your laugh, and your eagle eyes are appreciated more than you know. Thank you Erika, for taking the reins—I really don't know what I would've done without you these past few months. Thank you for shepherding this project—your communication skills are something to behold. Your courage and positive outlook always brighten my days.

Thank you to photographer and friend, Mark Tanner. Your distinctive touch is evident in every image.

INDEX